GOODS VEHICLE
OPERATORS'
LICENSING

GOODS VEHICLE
OPERATORS'
LICENSING

R S THORNTON

KOGAN
PAGE

All extracts from Government publications, Statutes, Statutory instruments, Law Reports, Transport Tribunal appeal decisions and other official sources are reproduced with the permission of the Controller of Her Majesty's Stationery Office.

First published in 1988 by
Kogan Page Ltd
120 Pentonville Road
London N1 9JN

Printed and bound in Great Britain by Mackays Limited, Chatham, Kent

British Library Cataloguing in Publication Data

Thornton, R.S.
    Goods vehicle operators' licensing, a
    complete guide to the law and procedures.
    1. Great Britain. Commercial vehicles.
    Operators' licences. Law
    I. Title
    344.103'946

ISBN 1-85091-479-6

Contents

Introduction

The present system of Goods Operator Licensing was introduced by the Transport Act 1968 (referred to from now on as 'the 1968 Act'), in compliance with the recommendations of the Report of the Geddes Committee on Carrier Licensing, published in 1965. The central recommendations of that Report, namely that quantity control of goods vehicles should be abandoned in favour of a stricter quality control, was accepted and incorporated in the 1968 Act, with appropriate provision, in section 93, for transition from one system to the other. Section 71, which retained an element of quantity control in the shape of special authorisations for the use of large vehicles on journeys over 100 miles, was never implemented, and the relevant provisions were finally repealed by the Transport Act 1980 (Schedule 9 Pt II).

The operator licensing system as it now exists is based essentially on considerations of road safety and responsible operation, through insistence on good repute (or 'fitness'), the professional competence, and the financial standing of the applicant, as well as the arrangements for proper maintenance of the vehicles, and for ensuring compliance with the law relating to overloading of vehicles and drivers' hours. Many of these provisions formed part of the legislation governing Carrier Licensing – principally the Road and Rail Traffic Act 1933, as consolidated in the Road Traffic Act 1960 – and were taken over and modified in the 1968 Act. It is not intended to relate the history of carrier licensing, which is admirably summarised in the Geddes Report itself, nor to analyse the changes which were made in the process of the enactment of the 1968 Act. The aim of this book is to describe in detail the system of the 1968 Act as amended to date.

The Licensing Authority for each Traffic Area must refuse applications for licences if any of the requirements laid down in the Act is not satisfied, and they have wide powers of revocation, suspension or curtailment of licences if operators fail to maintain adequate standards (see Chapter 7). In addition, by amendments to the 1968 Act implemented in June 1984 (by the Transport Act 1982), certain requirements as to the environmental suitability of operating centres may be taken into account on the grant or variation of licences (see Chapter 5).

Most decisions of Licensing Authorities made in compliance with the provisions of the Act and the Regulations made thereunder are subject to appeal to the Transport Tribunal by one party or another, and the decisions of the Tribunal have contributed significantly – sometimes indeed decisively – to the body of substantive and procedural law which governs this jurisdiction. The object of this book is to set out the provisions of the Act and Regulations, as amended from time to time, with particular reference to the decisions of the Tribunal, most of which are not published in any readily accessible form. Some of the appeal decisions referred to, dealing with issues of principle which still apply today, were given before the relevant parts of the Act came into operation in 1970. Any appeal judgement cited which bears a date earlier than 1970 may be assumed to have been decided on those parts of the 1960 Act which are analogous to the 1968 Act. As will be seen, the Transport Tribunal has been reconstituted as from September 1986, and new rules have been made which were effective from 1 October 1986, and which differ in some particulars from the previously existing rules.[1]

However, it is not anticipated that the principles upon which the Tribunal act, and the way in which they approach their task, will be altered, and the decisions made by the predecessor body will be no less authoritative or persuasive than before, on issues where the substantive law remains the same.

Of course, in addition to the orders of the Licensing Authority which may be appealed to the Transport Tribunal, holders of operators' licences may be prosecuted in magistrates' courts for offences against the Act and Regulations, with the usual rights of appeal to the Crown Court or the High Court as appropriate. Prosecutions may be brought by the Police, by County Trading Standards Officers, or by the Licensing Authority himself through his enforcement staff. Such proceedings, although forming the essential core of the enforcement system, are not directly relevant to the licensing functions of the Authority, and will not be dealt with in this book.

The Licensing Authority

The post of Licensing Authority for Goods Vehicles in each Traffic Area is held, by virtue of his office, by the person whom the Secretary of State has appointed as Traffic Commissioner for that Area.[2] When exercising his functions under the Transport Act 1968 as amended, the Traffic Commissioner is known, and is referred to in the legislation as 'the Licensing Authority'. As such he acts under the

[1] The Transport Tribunal Rules 1965 SI 1965 No 1687 as amended.
[2] Under section 3 of the Transport Act 1985, replacing and amending previous statutes.

general direction of the Secretary of State: 1968 Act section 59(2). The Licensing Authority is not, however, a civil servant, and is not answerable, so far as his statutory licensing functions are concerned, to the Secretary of State or any departmental officer. The Secretary of State will not as a rule answer parliamentary questions on the individual decision of Licensing Authorities, which can be challenged only on appeal to the Tribunal or the courts. The Secretary of State appoints Deputies to the Traffic Commissioner, who act as Deputy Licensing Authorities, and when so acting exercise all the powers of the Licensing Authority. Any reference in these pages to the Licensing Authority acting in that capacity must be read as applying equally to his Deputy or Deputies. He and they, being 'creatures of statute', can do only what Parliament has expressly authorised them to do, and cannot assume any general power to act upon their own view of what the public interest requires.[3]

The Licensing Authority performs both administrative and judicial functions, in the granting and variation of operators' licences, and in the monitoring of operators' performance, and the enforcement of standards. His function is sometimes termed 'quasi-judicial', which means that it consists, in part at least, of considering and weighing evidence and coming to decisions upon it, in accordance with principles and procedures laid down in statutes or regulations; and that his decisions are subject to appeal to an appellate tribunal and if necessary to the courts.

The Licensing Authority is also a 'tribunal' under the general supervision of the Council on Tribunals set up under the Tribunals and Inquiries Act 1971. However, the Licensing Authority is not strictly a 'court', and there are neither formal pleadings nor strict rules of evidence, the essential principle being that any Public Inquiry is conducted with an open mind and in a judicial manner. He must act in accordance with the principles of natural justice, and cannot deprive an operator of his licence without giving him the opportunity of a hearing.[4] (The latter rule is now subject to the specific provisions of the 1984 Regulations.) There is no power to take evidence on oath, and statements made in the course of an inquiry, whether by the Licensing Authority himself or any party, witness or advocate, do not enjoy absolute privilege.

In practice the majority of applications for licences and variations are routinely dealt with by the Licensing Authority's staff in his name and under his general guidance; he must take responsibility for all decisions made. Cases with unusual features would be referred to

---

[3] Appeal 1983 No U10 *L & P Traffic Services Ltd.*
[4] Appeal 1963 No Z101 *W L Pattinson:* Court of Appeal judgement at (1964) Traffic Cases 240.

him, and either determined in Chambers or listed for a Public Inquiry to be conducted by himself or by a Deputy Licensing Authority. There are statutory procedures for the publication of applications and the decisions taken, as well as of the dates when Public Inquiries will be held and of the applications, or other cases, to be heard there.

It has frequently been said that the Licensing Authority is both prosecutor and judge, as well as being the executive arm for investigation of the actions of operators. The Foster Committee,[5] which reported in November 1978, recommended that the function of directing investigations and deciding what cases should be brought to public inquiry, and which operators should be 'disciplined' and on what grounds, should be removed from the Licensing Authority and transferred to a senior official in the Traffic Area Office, whom they proposed to call the 'Registrar'. The Licensing Authority would have no foreknowledge of the cases which would come before him, nor would he see any of the office files or records, and would make decisions purely on the evidence placed before him in 'court'. It is fair to say that Deputy Licensing Authorities, who are part-time appointees paid fees for the days on which they sit, operate in a way broadly similar to that just described, except that they may well – and usually do – receive a briefing on the background of the individual operator concerned, and/or on the policy thought to be applicable to the case.

The recommendation of the Foster Committee on this point was seen, both by Licensing Authorities and the industry, as altogether changing the responsibilities of the Licensing Authority and the relationship between Traffic Areas and operators; it was not accepted by the Government and is perhaps unlikely to be followed up.[6]

Licensing Authorities are appointed by the Secretary of State partly from the ranks of serving civil servants and partly through public advertisement, in roughly equal proportions. Their numbers were reduced in 1984 from eleven to eight,[7] following a redrawing of Traffic Area boundaries, and their compulsory retiring age was reduced from 70 to 65 by the Transport Act 1985 (save for existing office-holders). Each Licensing Authority is required by section 59(3) of the Act to make to the Secretary of State an annual report of his proceedings, containing particulars of such matters as the Secretary of State may direct.

---

[5] An Independent Committee of Inquiry into Road Haulage Operator Licensing, under the chairmanship of Professor Christopher Foster.

[6] The Report, which was very comprehensive, contained a large number of other recommendations, many of which were adopted.

[7] One of whom is the Licensing Authority for two Areas separately.

CHAPTER 1

Principles of Licensing

Section 60 of the 1968 Act makes it an offence, punishable by a fine not exceeding £1000,[1] for a person to use a goods vehicle on a road for the carriage of goods (a) for hire or reward, or (b) for or in connection with any trade or business carried on by him, except under an operator's licence. For this purpose a goods vehicle is a motor vehicle or trailer constructed or adapted for the carriage of goods, and having a plated weight exceeding 3.5 tons or (if it does not have a plated weight) an unladen weight exceeding 30 cwt. Classes of vehicles exempt from licensing are listed in Schedule 5 to the Goods Vehicles (Operators' Licences, Qualifications and Fees) Regulations 1984 SI 1984 No 176 reproduced as Appendix A at the end of this book.

Sections 62 and 64 of the 1968 Act set out the information to be supplied with an application for a licence and the requirements which have to be satisfied in order to obtain a grant. An applicant for a licence must apply to the Licensing Authority for each Traffic Area in which, if the licence is granted, he will have one or more operating centres; if he will have operating centres in more than one Traffic Area, he must apply separately to each one; if he will have more than one operating centre in the same Traffic Area, one application and one licence will cover them all. 'Operating centre' is now defined, in section 52 of the Transport Act 1982, as 'the base or centre at which the vehicle is normally kept'. The subject is fully discussed in Chapters 3 and 5.

Authorised and specified vehicles

Section 61(1) of the 1968 Act sets out the rules defining 'authorised' and 'specified' vehicles and their categorisation under the licensing system. An operator or would-be operator is advised[2] to apply for

---

[1] Level 4 under the Criminal Justice Act 1982, as increased by the Criminal Penalties (increase) Order SI 1984 No 447.

[2] By paragraph 18 of the Department of Transport's publication *A Guide to Goods Vehicle Operators Licensing* (GV74).

more vehicles than he intends actually to use, at any rate in the immediate future. The total number of vehicles (including trailers) for which the licence is granted constitute the 'authorised' vehicles, and the number of vehicles actually used are known as the 'specified' vehicles; the difference between the two figures is called the 'margin'. On being granted his licence the operator 'specifies' ie registers with the Traffic Area, the motor vehicles (ie not including trailers) which he has in possession, and on which he will pay the requisite fees[3]. Specified vehicles are listed by registered number on a form (GV79A) which also records the year of registration, the plated or manufacturer's weight, and the body type. A windscreen disc is issued for each specified vehicle, showing the operator's name, the licence number and its expiry date, and the registered number of the vehicle. Different coloured discs are issued according as the licence is standard national, standard international or restricted (these terms are explained in detail on pp 15 – 17). Discs must be carried, and be kept legible, so long as the vehicles are specified on the licence. A vehicle may not be specified on more than one licence at a time: **section 61(5)**.

An operator may specify as many vehicles as are authorised by the licence; trailers are not individually specified. Every motor vehicle must be specified on the licence not later than one month after it is acquired by the licence-holder or comes into his possession under an agreement for hire-purchase, hire or loan: **section 61(3)**. He may use it during that month provided that he has a margin for it, ie it is within the total number of vehicles authorised by the licence. This provision in effect gives the operator a month's grace to specify a vehicle; it may also cause difficulty for enforcement officers, who will not normally know exactly when the vehicle was acquired. It is not unknown for an operator to hire vehicles in succession for periods of just under one month, and thus quite legally avoid the necessity to specify any of them.

Section 61(2) provides that a licence granted by one Licensing Authority does not authorise the use of any vehicle whose operating centre is outside the area of that Licensing Authority, for longer than a period of three months – two or more successive periods not separated from each other by at least three months being treated as a single period. A vehicle which is moved to an operating centre in another Traffic Area for more than three months should strictly, therefore, be licensed in that area.

---

[3] £20 on the grant of the licence and £5 per quarter for each vehicle specified: SI 1986 No 666 amending the Goods Vehicles (Operators' Licences, Qualifications and Fees) Regulations 1984 SI No 176.

Section 61(6) provides that if the Licensing Authority is informed that a specified vehicle has ceased to be used under the licence (other than temporarily), or is specified in another operator's licence, he may direct the removal of the vehicle from the first licence. As will be seen, such a direction is appealable by the licence-holder. Regulation 30(1) of the Goods Vehicles (Operators' Licences, Qualifications and Fees) Regulations 1984 SI No 176 requires the holder of a licence who ceases to use any specified vehicle to notify the Licensing Authority within 21 days and return the disc for cancellation and the licence for alteration. It nevertheless not infrequently happens that a licence-holder ceases to carry on business, and disposes of his vehicles, without informing the Licensing Authority. Failure to comply with Regulation 30(1) is an offence, by virtue of Regulation 33, for which the offender may be fined. A conviction for the offence is also a ground for revocation, suspension etc of the licence under section 69(4)(b)(iii)[4], so that the Licensing Authority may, after due notice to the licence-holder, formally revoke the licence.

Content of the application

The applicant must supply the information required by **section 62(2)**, that is to say 'a statement, giving such particulars as the authority may require' of the vehicles proposed to be used under the licence which he either owns or has on hire-purchase, hire or loan, or which he proposes to acquire in any of these ways, and also stating the number and type of trailers proposed to be used. ('Trailer' is not defined, but normally means a semi-trailer forming part of a combination, although it may also be a separate or 'drawbar' trailer.) In addition the Licensing Authority, under **section 62(4)**, may require the applicant to provide further information 'reasonably required for the discharge of his duties in relation to the application'.

The principal items of information – which are in practice supplied by way of answers to questions in the application form GV79 – relate to:

(i)   the facilities and arrangements for securing the proper maintenance of the vehicles;

(ii) the previous activities of the applicant in relation to a trade or business involving the operation of vehicles;

---

[4]   The Licensing Authority's powers of revocation etc are fully dealt with on p 113.

(iii) any convictions of the applicant or associated persons, eg other directors of a company, of a kind set out in section 69(4) of the Act[5], including convictions suffered after the date of the application;

(iv) the financial resources which are or are likely to be available to the applicant.

The Licensing Authority is also entitled to require information, in the case of a company applicant, on the names of the directors and officers of the company, and of any company of which the applicant company is a subsidiary: **section 62(4)(g)**. All such information is or may be evidence on which the Licensing Authority will determine whether the requirements of section 64(2) are met, and if it is not provided the Authority will be entitled (and perhaps bound) to refuse the application: see Appeal 1976 No N16 *A W and S J Caine.*

Since 1 June 1984, under the provisions of Schedule 4 to the Transport Act 1982[6], every application must include a statement giving such particulars as the Authority may require of each place in the area of the Authority which the applicant intends will be an operating centre for vehicles authorised under the licence: **section 69A(2)** of the 1968 Act as amended by the Schedule.

Consideration of the application

Having received the application, together with the relevant information, the Licensing Authority is required by **section 64(1)** to consider 'in every case' whether the three requirements of section 64(2)(a)(c) and (d) are satisfied. (Paragraph (b) was deleted by the Transport Act 1982 Schedule 6.) The requirements are as follows:

(a) that the applicant is a fit person to hold an operator's licence;

(c) that there will be satisfactory arrangements for ensuring compliance with the drivers' hours rules and that the vehicles will not be overloaded;

(d) that there will be satisfactory facilities and arrangements for maintaining the authorised vehicles in a fit and serviceable condition, *and that the place which is to be the operating centre for those vehicles is suitable for that purpose.*

---

[5] See pp 29 – 30 for details of these convictions.
[6] This Schedule inserted new sections 69A to 69G into the 1968 Act, to follow after section 69.

(The last 19 words of (d) were added by the Road Traffic Act 1974. Their significance will be fully discussed in Chapter 2.)

The Licensing Authority may also, if he thinks fit, consider a further requirement:

(e) that the provision of such facilities and arrangements as are mentioned in paragraph (d), *and of a suitable operating centre*, will not be prejudiced by reason of the applicant's having insufficient financial resources for that purpose.

(The words in italics were also added by the Road Traffic Act 1974.)

If the Licensing Authority decides, whether in the light of an objection[7] or otherwise, that any one of the requirements which he has taken into account is not satisfied he must refuse the application, but in any other case he must grant it[8], whether as applied for, or limited as to the type or number of vehicles, by virtue of section 67(3) which empowers the Licensing Authority to grant licences subject to either or both these limitations. Since the implementation of the environmental provisions of the Transport Act 1982 the obligation to grant is made subject to the provisions of sections 69B and 69E (see pages 42 – 43 for examination of these provisions).

Types of licence

Before considering the three requirements in detail it is necessary to refer to the further provisions relating to 'standard' and 'restricted' licences introduced by the Goods Vehicle Operators (Qualifications) Regulations 1977[9] as replaced and amended by the Goods Vehicles (Operators' Licences, Qualifications and Fees) Regulations 1984 SI 1984 No 176. The 1977 Regulations were made in order to enable the EEC Directive 74/561 on the admission of persons to the occupation of road haulage operator in national and international transport operations to be implemented in Great Britain, and came into operation on 29 September 1977. They provided that operators' licences granted so as to take effect on after 1 January 1978 should be divided into two classes, 'standard' and 'restricted', the former being further subdivided into 'national' and 'international'. In essence, a standard licence would entitle the holder to carry goods for hire or reward; a restricted licence would cover the carriage of the holder's

---

[7] For objections, see pp 52 ff.

[8] The Licensing Authority does not have a general discretion to grant or refuse an application in accordance with his view of the public interest: Appeal 1983 No U10 *L & P Traffic Services Ltd*.

[9] SI 1977 No 1462.

own goods only. Regulation 3(6) of the 1977 Regulations made it a punishable offence to use a goods vehicle under a restricted licence for carrying goods for hire or reward, and provided that the licence of an operator convicted of this offence twice within 5 years must be revoked under section 69 of the 1968 Act.[10] Regulation 3(7) made it an offence to use a goods vehicle under a standard *national* licence for carrying goods for hire or reward on international transport operations.[11]

To the requirements of section 64(2) these Regulations added three further requirements, applicable to standard licences only, namely that the applicant must:

(f)   be of good repute;
(g)   have appropriate financial standing;
(h)   be professionally competent.

In relation to the section 64(2) requirements, as they apply to applications for standard licences, (f) overlaps (a) 'fit person', (g) probably replaces (e) 'financial resources', and (h) is a new requirement altogether. Regulation 5 of the 1977 Regulations provides that the Licensing Authority 'shall refuse' to grant a standard operator's licence unless he is satisfied that the applicant fulfils the three requirements (f), (g) and (h). All the requirements, for both restricted and standard licences, will be considered in the following chapters.

Continuity

In order to secure that an applicant for 'renewal' of an existing licence is not prejudiced by possible delays in the processing of his application, **section 67(4)** of the 1968 Act provides that if his application is lodged before the existing licence expires,[12] the latter will continue in force until the fresh application, or any appeal arising out of it, is determined, without prejudice to the exercise meanwhile by the Licensing Authority of his powers of revocation etc under section 69. Section 67(4) also provides, as a further protection for the applicant, that if renewal is refused and the applicant appeals, the licence remains valid pending the appeal. If the 'renewal' is refused, the continuing licence will also be revoked.[13]

---

[10]   For powers of revocation etc see p 113.
[11]   For the definition of 'national' and 'international' see pp 15 – 17.
[12]   Licences are normally granted for 5 years, but the Licensing Authority may at discretion grant for a shorter period: section 67(3).
[13]   See Appeal 1985 No W24 *G B Hunt*.

A note on 'interim' grants and directions

To enable grants of licences to be made on a temporary or trial basis, or to enable operators to commence operating before all the preliminary steps for the grant of a licence have been completed, **section 67(5)** of the 1968 Act provides for an applicant for a licence to request the Licensing Authority to grant him, pending the decision on the application, 'an operator's licence expressed to continue in force until the date on which any licence granted on the application or on an appeal arising out of it is expressed to come into force, or if no licence is granted as aforesaid, until the application is refused'. Although the word 'interim' is not used in the section, licences granted under its terms are normally referred to as 'interim licences'.

Regulation 12 of SI 1984 No 176 requires an application to be lodged 9 weeks before the licence is to take effect, and this is therefore regarded as the average or 'par' time between application and decision. However, there may be special reasons why the applicant needs a licence earlier; or there may be unavoidable delays in processing the application, eg in providing accounts as evidence of financial standing, or because objections and/or representations have been lodged which have to be disposed of. The grant of an 'interim' licence is wholly within the Licensing Authority's discretion, and there can be no appeal against refusal. It will be granted only for vehicles in the possession of the applicant, and special 'interim' discs will be issued.[14] An interim standard licence will not be granted without evidence of professional competence, and *prima facie* evidence of good repute and financial standing may be required.[15] The request can be made only if an application for a licence has been lodged, but it is itself made informally; it is not published or made open to objection. The 'substantive' application will of course be processed in the usual way.

Strictly, an interim licence is not granted for a fixed term, but lasts until the substantive application is either granted – on appeal if necessary – or refused. It is perhaps uncertain whether, if an application in respect of which an interim licence has been granted is refused on substantive consideration, the holder can nevertheless keep the interim licence alive by appealing. Because of the possibility that an interim licence, granted as such, might have its life prolonged beyond the refusal of the substantive application, Licensing Authorities do not normally grant interim licences until the period for representations on environmental grounds – 21 days from the statutory

---

[14] The fee is £10 per vehicle: SI 1986 N0 666.
[15] Appeal 1984 No V2 *Michael John Mortimer* v. *RHA Ltd.*

advertisement – has expired. In addition, the applicant may be asked to provide evidence that the local authority will not object to the substantive application.

The Transport Tribunal had occasion to consider the status of 'interim' licences in Appeal 1986 No X29 *Kirk Brothers Ltd* v. *Macclesfield Borough Council & Others.* They emphasised that if the request for an 'interim' is granted, the whole of the application still remains to be determined, and that there has been as yet no opportunity for objections or representations against it; and indeed the Licensing Authority is not required to consider any of the matters specified in section 64 before granting the request. In the context of environmental objections to an application, where the question is whether the grant would result in material change from the position under an 'existing licence', an 'interim' does not rank as an existing licence for the purpose. In the appeal cited above the Tribunal said that if it were otherwise it would lead to 'the absurd situation that the grant of an interim licence without any opportunity for objection or representation could prevent the Licensing Authority from refusing an application which he would certainly have refused if he had not granted the interim licence'.

Section 68(5) provides that if an applicant for a variation so requests, a Licensing Authority may give an 'interim direction' (the word 'interim' is used in this section) granting the variation pending determination of the application. The same principles apply as on a request for an interim licence. In respect of variations relating to operating centres or environmental conditions (see pp 86 – 91 on environmental conditions) **section 69D (9)** provides for interim directions to be given in the same way as under section 68(5). Again, requests for interim directions do not have to be published and are not open to objection, but (especially in relation to environmental matters) Licensing Authorities are unlikely to grant interims while there is still time for environmental objections or representations to be lodged.

CHAPTER 2

Requirements for an Operator's Licence

Under section 64(2)

(1) 'Fit person' (section 64 (2) (a))

The fitness of an individual, partnership or company to hold an operator's licence is to be judged in the light of the matters of which particulars may be required to be given under sections 62(4)(d) and (e), that is to say any previous activities of the applicant, his partners or co-directors as the case may be, and in particular any 'relevant convictions' of any such persons – ie those listed in section 69(4) of the Act.

Appeal 1972 No J4 *Spinks Interfreight Ltd* v. *Road Haulage Association Ltd* is instructive for a detailed examination and discussion of the previous record of the directors of an applicant company, and the tests to be applied in deciding whether such activities made the company other than a 'fit person'. The Licensing Authority had refused to grant the company a licence for 50 vehicles and 88 trailers. The company itself was a newcomer to the haulage industry, but its directors had all been involved with other companies carrying on businesses which operated vehicles, most of which came to a 'disastrous end' for financial and other reasons. The Transport Tribunal reached the conclusion on the evidence that they 'were unable to say that they were not satisfied' that the company was a fit person, the double negative perhaps indicating the degree of doubt in their minds.

The activities and/or convictions under consideration must have taken place before the application (section 62(4)(e)) and there is therefore no room for the application of the 'fit person' test as such to an existing licence-holder so as to affect the continuance of this licence, except on the occasion of a renewal – which is in law a fresh application. The Licensing Authority may raise the issue himself, or it may be raised by a statutory objector under section 63(3).[1] It will

---

[1]   For objections by statutory objectors, see pp 46 ff.

not infrequently arise on an application for renewal, when the previous record of the operator may come under scrutiny. The 'fit person' test goes to the root of the question whether the applicant should be allowed to have an operator's licence at all; it is not strictly relevant to such considerations as the number of vehicles which should be authorised or the length of term to be granted.

The appeal decisions suggest that something more than bad operation or neglect of maintenance in the past is required to prove unfitness,[2] especially as it is essentially a once-for-all judgment which may have the effect of disqualifying the applicant from ever holding a licence.[3] Some instances may be given. In Appeal 1974 No L21 *Albert Robson*, an applicant who had held himself out to be a director of a non-existent company and operated as such company was held not to be a fit person; in Appeal 1977 No 011 *G & D Services* it was stated that 'anybody who is incompetent to run a haulier's business is not fit to hold an operator's licence', the fact of incompetence having been found by a magistrates' court. In Appeal 1978 No P16 *J M Schofield*, on a finding (on the evidence as it then stood) that the operator had failed to keep records and then lied about the matter at a Public Inquiry, it was said that he would not be a fit person.

It will be noted from these decisions that 'previous activities' may include conduct of a kind which is subversive of the licensing system or its proper administration, without there being any conviction under section 62(4)(e). In Appeal 1971 No H5 *Thomas Small*, the applicant had used vehicles without an operator's licence, although he had not been convicted of this offence. The Tribunal considered the argument that such conduct could not be considered as an 'activity' under section 62(4)(d) unless it had been the subject of a conviction, and said: 'In our view this argument is unsound. Conduct in the course of carrying on a haulier's business is not excluded from being a relevant activity under section 62(4)(d) merely because it might have been the subject of a conviction to which regard could be had under section 62(4)(e)'. Again, it appears inferentially from observations of the Transport Tribunal in Appeal 1984 No V7 *Wilkinson Freight (UK) Ltd* that fraudulent conduct without conviction might make a person unfit to hold a licence: ' . . . in the absence of any conduct amounting to fraudulent trading, Mr Wilkinson's involvement in the liquidation . . . cannot render him unfit to hold an operator's licence.'

---

[2] See Appeals 1970 No G4 *W A Glendinning Ltd*, 1973 No K27 *Stancrest Transport Ltd*.
[3] But see Appeal 1984 No V15 *Peter Hooper t/a Petran International*, where the Tribunal observed that the person's conduct between the date of the offence and the hearing of the application should be taken into account.

It is perhaps questionable whether convictions which are outside those listed in section 69(4) could strictly qualify as 'previous activities' so as to make the person concerned not a fit person, because the listing (by reference) of specific convictions in section 62(4)(e) might raise the presumption that any convictions *not* so listed were excluded. It would however be anomalous if conduct without conviction could affect fitness, while a conviction for the same conduct did not; and the better view must be that a conviction is *a fortiori* relative to conduct, or at least may be evidence of such conduct.

The introduction of the requirement of 'good repute' for standard licences from 1 January 1978 has to some extent subsumed or replaced the 'fit person' requirement, although as will be seen there are some important differences, the principal one being that a standard licence may (indeed must) be revoked if the Licensing Authority at any time determines that the licence-holder has ceased to be of good repute.

(2) Compliance with drivers' hours and weight limit (Section 64(2)(c))

The application form GV79 requires the applicant to declare that he will make proper arrangements to ensure that the rules on drivers' hours are observed and that vehicles are not overloaded. In respect of a new application, the Licensing Authority has no practical alternative to accepting the declaration as a statement of intention for the future which, if not fulfilled, will give grounds for 'disciplinary' action under section 69. If the application is for a renewal, or if the applicant has held a licence previously, his record may be looked at, and if he has had convictions for overloading or for breach of drivers' hours or tachograph regulations, the Licensing Authority may require further evidence to satisfy him as to the future.

(3) Facilities and arrangements for maintenance (Section 64(2)(d))

The requirement to maintain the authorised vehicles in a fit and serviceable condition at all times is one of the central obligations of the licensed goods vehicle operator. The undertaking which the operator gives on the application form is not that there *are* but that there *will be* satisfactory facilities and arrangements for this purpose.

21

The applicant is asked to state whether he will carry out his own 'preventive maintenance inspections' or whether they will be carried out by a garage or other third party (eg another licensed operator) on contract. In either case he will be required to state the proposed frequency of such inspections in terms of time and mileage. His replies to these (and other) questions in the application form will or may be treated as statements of intention within section 69(1)(c), failure to fulfil which may give grounds for action against the licence (see Chapter 7, p000).

The evidence to support the statement of intention will normally be either (i) a Vehicle Examiner's report on the facilities in the case of 'own maintenance', or (ii) a copy of the agreement with the garage or other third party in the case of contracted out maintenance. In perhaps the majority of cases in category (i) it may not be possible to have the facilities inspected in time,[4] and the Licensing Authority may decide to grant the licence and rely on the applicant's assurances and, if necessary, take retrospective action if the report eventually proves unfavourable; or he may if so requested grant an 'interim' licence with a view to inspection before substantive grant.

On renewal applications the statement of intention is normally accepted as adequate unless there is a record of unsatisfactory maintenance – evidenced by GV9 prohibitions, failures on annual tests or adverse technical reports – during the currency of the previous licence. If the record is bad enough the application might be refused on 'fit person' grounds,[5] although except in extreme cases this would not be done without a Public Inquiry. It is of course open to the Licensing Authority to grant for a limited period under section 67(3) on a probationary or trial basis – provided, however, that the power to limit the duration of a licence under section 67(3) is exercised to ensure that the requirements mentioned in section 64(2) will be satisfied, and not as a penalty imposed in respect of the applicant's past failure to comply with his obligations: Appeal 1975 No M8 *National Carriers Ltd.*

The previous record of the applicant may of course be relevant as indicating the probability (or lack of it) that maintenance will be properly carried out in the future; this will be so particularly in cases where the operator in question has had previous warnings or has made promises as to improvement which have have not been kept. In Appeal 1970 No G10 *D Clemetson* (a case of refusal to renew) the Transport Tribunal said: 'Most of the appellant's record relates to the unsatisfactory way in which he has maintained his vehicles. Had we been satisfied that the appellant had turned over a new leaf and

---

[4]   ie within the 9 weeks mentioned in Regulation 12 of SI 1984 No 176.
[5]   See Appeal 1973 No K24 *E C Cases Ltd*.

that there would be satisfactory facilities and arrangements for maintaining his vehicles in the future, we would not have held him unfit to hold an operator's licence merely by reason of his past shortcomings regarding maintenance.' Similar principles have been stated in two cases in which the applications were to vary the licences by adding vehicles – which, the Tribunal observed, were to be dealt with on the same basis as renewals.[6]

(4) Operating centre suitable for purpose (Section 64(2)(d))

As has been noted, the Road Traffic Act 1974 added to section 64(2)(d) the requirement 'that the place which is to be the operating centre is suitable for that purpose'. As the immediately preceding passage relates to the maintenance of the authorised vehicles, the last five words might be interpreted as meaning 'suitable for the maintenance of the vehicles', but successive Tribunal decisions have put beyond doubt that they mean 'suitable for the purpose of an operating centre', and further, that the wording does not import any element of environmental suitability, whatever may have been the intentions of the drafters of the amendment. In four appeals heard in the same month (February 1976), namely

1975 No M15 *RHA Ltd* v *A Cash and A McCall*
1975 No M16 *RHA Ltd* v *D Sheridan and F Bell*
1975 No M17 *RHA Ltd* v *J Shepherd*
1975 No M18 *Owen House Limited*

the Tribunal stated two principles governing the interpretation of the 1974 amendment, that is to say:

(i) the definition of 'operating centre' in section 92(1) of the 1968 Act[7] as 'the base or centre from which the vehicles are or are intended to be normally used' meant the place where control of the vehicles is exercised, or in other words 'where the operator gives his orders which govern the manner in which goods are to be carried by his vehicles on roads', and the suitability of the operating centre is to be judged on that basis, and not in relation to the maintenance of the vehicles, which may or may not be kept there;

(ii) not only did 'suitability' not import any environmental connection, but a Licensing Authority was not entitled to take environmental considerations into account at all. 'Whether the use of premises in a residential area for commercial purposes would be detrimental to the environment is a matter to be dealt with under the legislation relating to town and country planning . . . In considering

---

[6]   1973 No K3 *Southern Linen Services Limited*;
     1973 No K22 *William Davidson*.
[7]   Now amended: see p 25.

the suitability of an operating centre a Licensing Authority should confine his attention to the premises in question and decide whether they are suitable in themselves for the purposes for which the applicant for the licence proposes to use them. Examples of relevant considerations would be the physical characteristics of the premises and the size of the operator's fleet with the consequential effect upon the number of persons to be employed at the operating centre. A Licensing Authority could not be expected to regard as suitable an allotment shed without heating, lighting or sanitation, nor would he be likely to regard a two-up two-down cottage as a suitable operating centre for a fleet of 100 vehicles.'[8]

Despite *Cash and McCall* local authorities continued to lodge objections on planning or environmental grounds in reliance on the amended section 64(2)(d), but the doors were gradually closed, as the following series of appeal decisions illustrates:

(i) Appeal 1977 No 03 *Livestock Sales Transport Ltd* v. *Tunbridge Wells Borough Council.* A planning permission as interpreted by the local planning authority limited the use of certain repair facilities to 4 vehicles. It was *held* that the licence should be granted for 8 vehicles as applied for 'leaving the operator to ensure that the planning permission is not contravened'.

(ii) Appeal 1979 No Q10 *A F Mansfield* v. *Leicester City Council.* Use of the applicant's council house as an operating centre was prohibited by planning law and contrary to his tenancy agreement. The Tribunal said: '. . the three matters [namely planning, housing and operator licensing] seem to us to be entirely independent and the mere fact that he may run into difficulties over getting two of them is no reason why he should not have his operator's licence.'

(iii) Appeal 1982 No T13 *Cameron Shuttering Ltd* v. *Tunbridge Wells Borough Council.* Use of the operating centre as such was contrary to planning law; the Council had served an enforcement notice, an appeal from which had been dismissed; and they were prosecuting the company for breach of the notice. The Licensing Authority refused the application on the ground that a place which the operator was being prosecuted for using as an operating centre could not, by that very fact, be 'suitable'. The Tribunal allowed the operator's appeal, saying 'In our judgment premises may well be suitable for use as an operating centre within the meaning of the Transport Act 1968 although their use as such would be unlawful as being in breach of planning law or bye-law.'

---

[8]   Appeal 1976 no M15 *RHA Ltd* v. *A Cash and A McCall*

In the *Cameron Shuttering* appeal the Tribunal added that when section 52 of the Transport Act 1982 came into force, the changes which it brought about 'might well lead the Tribunal to different conclusions in a future case where the facts were similar'. The changes referred to, which became effective on 1 June 1984, will be fully considered later, but it is relevant at this point to note that objections may still be lodged on the grounds of general (ie other than environmental) unsuitability of the operating centre, under the new definition in section 52 of the 1982 Act, namely that it is the 'base or centre where the vehicle is normally kept'. The *environmental* suitability of the operating centre can be challenged only under the new provisions, sections 69A to 69G of the 1968 Act, but its *general* suitability could be the subject of objection under section 64(2)(d), if for instance its use as such gave rise to traffic hazards or constituted a threat to road safety. Indeed, if a statutory objector, eg a highway authority or the police, wishes to challenge the suitability of an operating centre on any grounds other than strictly environmental ones, it must lay its objection under section 63.

In Appeal 1985 No W30 *Strathkelvin District Council* v. *Fife Forwarding Company Ltd,* the Transport Tribunal said: 'For many years prior to the introduction of environmental considerations it was necessary for Licensing Authorities to take into account road safety in determining whether the proposed operating centre was suitable for the purpose, and local authorities and chief officers of police did on occasions raise road safety as an objection under section 63. Although the matter does not arise for decision on this Appeal our provisional view is that road safety does not fall within the words "environmental grounds" or "environmental conditions" which would appear to govern all objections and representations under section 69.'

In Appeal 1986 No X29 *Kirk Brothers Ltd* v. *Macclesfield Borough Council, Cheshire County Council and Others*, the Licensing Authority had refused the application on the grounds (amongst others) that the use of the proposed operating centre would be likely to cause a traffic hazard, in that the only means of ingress to and egress from it, for authorised vehicles, was directly from or onto a busy public road. Although the ground, both for the decision, and the dismissal of the appeal, was that the operating centre was unsuitable under section 64(2)(d), this does not mean that the effect of the authorised vehicles on public roads in general will always be a relevant consideration under that section. In Appeal 1987 No Y17 *Scorpio International Limited* v. *Lancashire County Council and South Ribble Borough Council,* the Tribunal said that while the considerations relevant to suitability under section 64(2)(d) may include public safety, a Licensing Authority should take into account the suitability only of private roads linking the operating centre to the public roads, and not the suitability of public roads themselves. They added that it was the responsibility of the highway authority to make such improvements in the public highway, or impose such restrictions on vehicle movements as it thinks fit.

(5) Adequacy of financial resources (Section 64(2)(e))

This is a discretionary requirement in that the Licensing Authority need only consider it if he thinks fit. It is also a limited one since the Authority need be satisfied only that the requirements under (d), ie maintenance of the vehicles and provision of a suitable operating centre, will not be prejudiced by reason of the applicant's having insufficient financial resources for the purpose. It is probable that very few applications have been refused on this ground, and since the introduction of the 'appropriate financial standing' test for standard licences it has perhaps become a dead letter. There are however two appeal decisions which relate to this particular requirement: the first is Appeal 1971 No H1 *F R Bullen*, the second Appeal 1984 No V4 *D W Briggs (Plant Hire) Limited,* in which the application was for a restricted licence.

In *Bullen* it was said that the facilities and arrangements for maintenance 'do not fall to be paid for in the first instance out of the receipts on the business; they must be provided out of working capital, with the hope that the working capital will in due course be serviced out of the receipts'. This was said with reference to the appellant's argument – one which is still heard from time to time – that if he was allowed more vehicles to earn money with he would be able to make better arrangements for their maintenance.[9]

In *Briggs* the licensing Authority had refused the restricted licence application primarily on the ground that the applicant was not a fit person, but had also found that the operators had insufficient financial resources to ensure proper maintenance of the vehicles. The Tribunal said as to this issue: 'The record of the previous companies suggested that the directors of the appellants were not good at managing cash flow problems. The absence of any working capital to withstand such problems, so frequently encountered in these days, would mean that the appellants were trading on an unacceptable hand-to-mouth basis.'

---

[9]   For an appeal in which this argument met with some success, see p 117.

Section 64(5) provides that in exercising his functions in relation to this requirement a Licensing Authority may be assisted by an assessor drawn from a panel appointed by the Secretary of State. As will be seen, there is no corresponding provision in the Regulations relating to 'appropriate financial standing', and it would seem that the section 64(5) provision would not entitle the Licensing Authority to the assistance of an assessor in that connection.

Special requirements for standard licences.

As already noted, an operator intending to carry goods for hire or reward, even occasionally, must have a 'standard' licence. It is primarily for the operator to decide whether he requires a standard or restricted licence and to make the appropriate application. If it appears on the face of the application or the supporting documentation that a restricted licence would not authorise the proposed operation, the Traffic Area Office will probably raise a query with the applicant, and/or the Licensing Authority may refuse to grant a restricted licence where a standard licence is obviously required (eg for a general haulier or furniture removal firm). There is no express power to refuse an application on these grounds, and it is arguable that provided the requirements of section 64 are met, the Licensing Authority must grant the application, but with a clear warning that the licence-holder must keep within the limits of the restricted licence. Most Licensing Authorities in such circumstances would probably refuse the application, on the ground that knowingly to grant an inappropriate licence could amount to condoning unauthorised operation, and might be said to lead the applicant into a trap. In Appeal 1982 No T19 *Wessex Waste Disposal Limited* the Licensing Authority, after a Public Inquiry where the law applicable to the uncontested facts was fully discussed, refused to grant a restricted licence on the ground that the operations – basically the removal of sludge and animal waste from cesspits and other places for resale to farmers – contained an element of 'hire or reward'. The Transport Tribunal did not consider the question of the Licensing Authority's right to refuse, but reversed the decision on the merits, holding that on the facts the operators became the owners of the material as soon as they had collected it, and were therefore carrying their own goods, for which a restricted licence was appropriate.

Difficult questions may still arise in these and other fields, the solution of which may depend on close examination of the details of the operation, for instance at what point ownership of the goods changes hands, or whether the charge for a service does or does not include any element of payment for the carriage of the goods.

27

Note: **National and International**

Regulation 4(3) of the Goods Vehicles (Operators' Licences, Qualifications and Fees) Regulations 1984 SI No 176 provides that standard licences may authorise goods vehicles to be used for the carriage of goods (a) on both international and national operations, or (b) on national transport operations only. Regulation 4(4)(b) requires each standard licence to state on its face whether it covers both international and national transport operations or national transport operations only. Licences are referred to as 'standard international' (SI) and 'standard national' (SN) respectively.

The 1977 and 1984 Regulations defined a national transport operation as a transport operation involving the use, for carrying goods for hire or reward, of a goods vehicle on a journey in the United Kingdom only; and an international transport operation as one involving the use, for carrying goods for hire or reward, of a goods vehicle on a journey which takes place in part in the United Kingdom and in part elsewhere.

The Goods Vehicles (Operators' Licences, Qualifications and Fees) (Amendment)(No 2) Regulations 1986 SI No 1391 redefined 'international transport operation' as having the same meaning as in the 1974 Council Directive (ie 74/561) and deleted the definition of 'national transport operation' from the 1984 Regulations. Council Directive 74/561 contains no definition of 'international transport operation', and the meaning of this expression can only be inferred, perhaps from the 'syllabus' for the international examination for professional competence set out in part B of the Annex, where the expression used is 'the transport of goods by road between member States and between the Community and non-member countries . . .'.

It is perhaps reasonably self-evident what international operations are, despite the absence of a definition. Whether the amending Regulations were intended to achieve this result or not, it seems that the Department of Transport, at least, no longer regards a standard international licence as being required by the operator of a tractor which tows trailers to and from UK ports for unaccompanied transit overseas without itself leaving the country. The statement in the Department's *Guide to Goods Vehicle Licensing* (GV74) to the effect that an international licence is required for this purpose has been removed. Any remaining uncertainty must be of some concern to operators, since it is an offence to carry goods on a standard national licence in circumstances where an international licence is required, and the licence itself may also be at risk. However, it is at least unlikely that any enforcement agency would take action to bring the matter before the courts.

The requirements examined

(i) Good Repute

Paragraph 9(2) of the Goods Vehicle Operators (Qualifications) Regulations 1977 SI No 1462 provided as follows:

'For the purpose of determining whether or not a person is of good repute regard shall be had in particular to the existence and number of any relevant convictions relating to him during the period of 5 years ending with the date on which the matter falls to be determined.'

This was the definition from 29 September 1977, when these Regulations came into operation, until 21 December 1980, when the Amendment Regulations 1980 SI No 1787 became effective, from which date the provisions read as follows:

'For the purpose of determining whether or not a person is of good repute regard shall be had to any matter, including a conviction for an offence, appearing to relate to fitness to hold a standard operator's licence or, as the case may be, to be a transport manager, and in particular to the existence and number of any specified convictions relating to the person, or any partner, employee or agent of the person, or in the case of a company, any officer of the company, during the period of 5 years ending with the date on which the matter falls to be determined.'

There is no essential difference between the definitions of 'relevant convictions' and 'specified convictions' in the respective Regulations, only the reference to 'transport manager' is transferred from the definition to the substantive provision, and convictions of partners, employees and agents are added. In both provisions the time limit is set at 5 years ending with the date on which the matter falls to be determined. This limitation was not repeated in the 1984 provisions, set out below, and the exact meaning of 'the date on which the matter falls to be determined' need not be considered. The Goods Vehicles (Operators' Licences, Qualifications and Fees) Regulations 1984 SI No 176, which came into effect on 1 June 1984, replaced *in toto* the 1977 Regulations as amended. Paragraph 1 of Schedule 6 to the 1984 Regulations provides as follows:

'1. (1) In determining whether an individual is of good repute a Licensing Authority shall have regard to any matter, and in particular –

(a) relevant convictions of the individual and his employees and agents; and

(b) such other information as the authority may have as to his previous conduct, appearing to relate to his fitness to hold a licence.

(2) In determining whether a company is of good repute, a Licensing Authority shall have regard to all the material evidence and in particular to –

(a) relevant convictions of the company, its officers, employees and agents; and

(b) such other information as the authority may have as to the previous conduct of –

   (i) the company's officers, employees and agents appearing to relate to the company's fitness to hold a licence; and

   (ii) each of the company's directors, in whatever capacity, appearing to relate to the company's fitness to hold a licence.'

As already pointed out (see p 29), the scope of 'good repute', although relating ultimately to the fitness of persons or companies to hold a licence, is wider than that of 'fit person' under section 64(2)(a) of the 1968 Act, since at all relevant times the Licensing Authority has been required to have regard to matters other than the 'relevant' or 'specified' convictions mentioned in section 64(4). In Appeal 1980 No R11 *Wilma Keenan or McColl (t/a W K Transport)*, where the Tribunal were applying the unamended 1977 Regulations, the Licensing Authority had found the operator's transport manager not to be of good repute on the basis (largely) of a conviction for the forging of a blank test certificate, which was not a 'relevant conviction'. The Transport Tribunal observed that 'the task for the Licensing Authority is to reach a view on an individual's reputation in general having regard to all circumstances'. Accordingly they held that in addition to the relevant convictions 'it is left for the Authority to pay regard to any other fact or circumstance properly before it which may have a relevant bearing upon the repute of the individual under consideration' – which included the conviction in question.[10]

It will be seen that this does not claim to define 'good repute', and indeed begs the question as to what may have a relevant bearing on an individual's repute. In Appeal 1980 No R18 *T B Jackson (t/a Jackson's Transport)* the Tribunal examined the origin of the Regulation, and considered a definition proposed by the Licensing Authority, namely that it would apply to operators 'whom a sensible customer would not employ if he were in a position to know all about

---

[10] This decision was followed in Appeal 1981 No S7 *D & H Spence*, and in Appeal 1987 No Y29 *Terence Keith Bonner t/a TK Bonner Transport*, in which they stated that in the interests of clarity the term 'relevant conviction' should be used only in the strict sense of a conviction mentioned in section 69(4) of the 1968 Act.

them'. The Tribunal declined to accept 'the addition of the knowledgable customer to the fictitious company of the hypothetical tenant and the officious bystander', although they dismissed the appeal on the merits, holding that even one conviction for a particularly heinous offence could deprive a person of his good repute.

In such a case the Licensing Authority is not concerned with the reasons given by the convicting court for the conclusions it reached. In Appeal 1987 No Y6 *Expo Removals Ltd* the person who was the Managing Director, Transport Manager and principal shareholder of the company had been convicted of an offence of fraudulent evasion of the Hydrocarbon Oils Regulations by, in effect, extracting the marker dye from diesel fuel. The Licensing Authority revoked the company's licence on the ground that it was no longer of good repute by reason of the aforesaid conviction.[11] On appeal it was argued that the sentence imposed by the Crown Court, and the presumed or possible reasons for the particular sentence – namely that the Judge did not intend to put the company out of business – should be taken into account. The Tribunal did not accept that any such conclusion should be drawn, but added that in any case the Crown Court Judge's reasons for passing the sentences were irrelevant. They said: 'The Licensing Authority is not in any sense bound by the decision of the Crown Court Judge, who was performing an entirely different function. It was not for him to consider whether the appellants satisfied the statutory requirement to be of good repute contained in Regulation 5 of the 1984 Regulations; whereas the Licensing Authority was obliged by law to revoke the appellants' licence if it appeared to him that the requirement was no longer satisfied.' The appeal was dismissed on the merits.

The Tribunal in Appeal 1982 No T1 *Janet Murfitt* considered whether it should have appeared to the Licensing Authority that the licence-holder was no longer of good repute.[12] In reaching their conclusion that her good repute had not been lost, the Tribunal took account of various matters which they considered relevant:

(i) the degree of Mrs Murfitt's involvement in the conspiracy in relation to which she was convicted;

(ii) her conduct as a business woman and as a member of the community, as to both of which matters detailed evidence in her favour was submitted by reputable persons;[13]

---

[11] which was not, it should be noted, a 'relevant conviction' under section 69(4).
[12] Under reg 8(1) of the 1977 Regulations as amended, corresponding to Regulation 9(1) of the 1984 Regulations.
[13] But 'short formal written references are most unlikely to carry any weight': Appeal 1982 No T11 *M Dyer and A W H Cork (t/a M & B Transport)*.

(iii) the time which had elapsed since the commission of the offence and her conduct since that time.

The Tribunal held that 'it is her reputation today, and not at some past time, that matters', but after saying that viewing the evidence as a whole it did not appear to them that the appellant was not of good repute, they added: 'We express no view on what our answer would have been if we had been considering that question immediately following the conviction, or if today we had information as to the extent of her involvement in the conspiracy.' Another feature of the case which evidently influenced the Tribunal was that another person 'deeply involved in the conspiracy' was judged by the Deputy Licensing Authority to have rehabilitated himself by December 1981. The Tribunal observed that 'the disparity between the Deputy Licensing Authority's assessment of the repute of D F and that of the appellant cannot be justified'.

Since the Licensing Authority is bound to revoke a licence if the operator is no longer of good repute, he must do so (if at all) *on the first occasion* when the evidence would appear to require it. In Appeal 1982 No T3 *K M H Transport* v. *South Yorkshire Police* the Licensing Authority had curtailed a licence by reason of, amongst other things certain convictions of Mr H. In 1981 he refused an application by another company of which Mr H was a director, on the ground that by reason of the same convictions Mr H was not of good repute. The Tribunal, in allowing the appeal, said: 'It is to be observed that the Deputy Licensing Authority has no discretion once it appears to him that the licence-holder is not of good repute. We are driven to conclude that in 1978 the Deputy Licensing Authority did not consider that Mr H had ceased to be of good repute in January of that year. In our judgment it would be illogical and unfair to come to a different conclusion three years later.'

In Appeal 1982 No T11 *M Dyer & M W H Cork* the Tribunal added that 'by positive efforts a person may acquire a good reputation in the community long before convictions recorded against him become spent under the Rehabilitation of Offenders Act.'

As the Tribunal pointed out in *T B Jackson*, 'an applicant for a licence cannot know in advance whether he is of good repute for the purpose of the Regulations nor can a licence-holder know with certainty whether he is still of good repute.' The latter point is met, to some extent at least, by the requirement in Regulation 9(2) that the Licensing Authority must give written notice in advance to the licence-holder that he is considering revocation on this ground and afford him an opportunity to make representations and be heard at a Public Inquiry. As regards applications, it is anticipated that a

Licensing Authority before refusing an application on grounds of 'no good repute' would in all but very exceptional cases give the applicant an opportunity to show cause why it should not be refused.

(2) Appropriate financial standing

> 'Being of appropriate financial standing in relation to an applicant for, or holder of, a licence consists in having available sufficient financial resources to ensure the establishment and proper administration of the road transport undertaking carried on, or proposed to be carried on, under the licence.'[14]

As with good repute and professional competence (see next section) the Licensing Authority is bound to refuse to grant a standard licence unless satisfied that this requirement is met. Under Regulation 9(2), moreover, he must revoke the licence 'if it appears to him' at any time that the holder no longer satisfies the requirement. As already noted, there is no provision in the Regulations for the Licensing Authority to be assisted by a financial assessor in reaching his conclusion on these issues.

It is difficult to lay down any firm guiding principles as to what constitutes 'appropriate financial standing', except by reference to the definition quoted above. In Appeal 1983 No U9 *Rosswood Limited* v. *Road Haulage Association Ltd* the Tribunal laid emphasis on the word 'ensure', and said that Regulation 9(3) imposes a stringent financial test. It is perhaps worth noting that all the reported appeals from refusals based on the lack of appropriate financial standing[15] have been dismissed, except for Appeal 1983 No U10, which was remitted to the Licensing Authority for further hearing on other grounds, the Tribunal having held that certain procedures had not been correctly observed, and certain evidence wrongly admitted. (For discussion of this aspect of the matter, see p 41.)

(3) Professional competence

This is the only requirement peculiar to 'standard' licences and not matched by any of the requirements for 'restricted' licences, after the

---

[14] The Goods Vehicles (Operators' Licences, Qualifications and Fees) Regulations 1984 SI No 176, Schedule 6 para 2.
[15] 1982 No T17 *Ian Salmons;*
1982 No T22 *Earthmoving Services Ltd*;
1983 No U9 *Rosswood Ltd* v. *Road Haulage Assoc Ltd*;
1983 No U10 *L & P Traffic Services Ltd*;
1984 No V6 *Cooper Transport* v. *Road Haulage Assoc Ltd;*
1984 No V17 *Mervyn Charles King t/a M & C Transport.*

severance of the two types of licence by the Goods Vehicle Operators (Qualifications) Regulations 1977. For clarity it will be necessary to trace the progress of the relevant provisions through two amendments, as follows:

(i) the 1977 provisions, operative from 1 January 1978 to 1 June 1984;
(ii) the 1984 provisions, operative from 1 June 1984;
(iii) the 1986 amendment, operative from 1 May 1986.

The 1977 Regulations, at Regulation 5(1), required the Licensing Authority to refuse to grant a standard operator's licence unless he was satisfied that:

'(a) . . .
(b) . . .
(c) the applicant is himself professionally competent or will at all times during the currency of the licence have in his employment a transport manager who is of good repute and is professionally competent, or, if the operator has more than one operating centre and the licensing authority requires him to have more than one transport manager, such number of transport managers who are of good repute and professionally competent as are so required.'

'Transport manager' was defined in Regulation 2 as meaning 'a person who is, or is to be, employed in full-time employment by the applicant, or as the case may be, who is employed in full-time employment by the holder, in a position where he is responsible for the operation of vehicles used under the licence . . . '.

The professional competence of an individual could be established in one of three ways:

(i) by evidence that he was engaged in road transport operations before 1 January 1975 – popularly known as 'grandfather rights'; to be valid after 31 December 1979 he had to have a certificate to that effect issued by a licensing authority before that date;
(ii) by his holding a certificate of having passed an examination in the subjects listed in the Community Instrument (EEC Directive 74/561);
(iii) by his holding a certificate of competence, diploma or other qualification recognised by the Secretary of State.[16]

It is to be noted that a certificate issued on the basis of 'grandfather rights' bestows on the holder professional competence for both national and international operations, whether or not his or

---

[16] See Appendix B for a current list of these.

her relevant experience covered both fields. Separate examinations are prescribed for 'national' and 'international' qualification, and for a 'standard international licence' the person concerned must have passed both examinations, and not only the 'international' Part B.

Method (i) – grandfather rights – ceased to be available after the end of 1979, although attempts have been made from time to time to establish professional competence by evidence of operation before 1 January 1975, together with the plea that the certificate to that effect was not obtained in time (ie before 31 December 1979) because of postal delays, illness, absence abroad or mere forgetfulness. The Transport Tribunal has consistently upheld the Licensing Authorities in their refusal to accept such applicants as professionally competent.[17] Methods (ii) and (iii) are now the only ones open to establish professional competence. It may be noted that professional competence, once legally acquired, cannot be lost or taken away, notwithstanding that the individual concerned may be shown to be incompetent or negligent in performing his duties; his good repute may of course be called in question, if not directly, then indirectly by challenging the professional competence of his employer.

If an individual licence-holder is himself professionally competent, that is sufficient for a grant, even though he takes no direct part in the operation of the vehicles; he does not need to employ a professionally competent transport manager. He will of course as a licence-holder have to have adequate facilities and arrangements for the maintenance of the vehicles, and as such he bears the ultimate responsibility for any shortcomings as a result of reliance on third parties.[18] The latter proposition is true even if the licence-holder employs a competent transport manager, but allowance would be made for his having relied in good faith on competent people, and 'done his best'.[19]

A partnership applying for a standard licence may employ a transport manager, but if it does not it will qualify as professionally competent if one or more of the partners is professionally competent, and a partner who is so qualified is responsible for the operation of the vehicles used under the licence. In Appeal 1983 No U19 *P E Baker & D G Baker t/a Baker Haulage* the Transport Tribunal had to consider the interpretation of this provision. They said: 'In our

---

[17] Appeal 1980 No R22 *C A Johnson (t/a Glenton Antiques)*;
   Appeal 1981 No S22 *David Ringer Ltd*;
   Appeal 1983 No U1 *Finsbury Coaches Ltd*.

[18] There are numerous authorities for this essential principle. See, for example, Appeals 1966 No C63 *Wigmore Transport Ltd*, 1977 No 015 *Arthur & Co (Floorcoverings) Ltd*, 1978 No P18 *M F Gomm t/a Portway Skip Services*.

[19] Appeal 1973 No K25 *Bernard Master Group of Companies Ltd*. His best may of course not be good enough: see Appeal 1971 No H20 *Raymond Taylor*.

judgment a licensing authority faced by this kind of application should answer the following questions in deciding whether the partner with a certificate of competence is responsible for the operation of the vehicles used:

(1) What work is required of the partner responsible for the operation of the vehicles? It hardly needs emphasis that driving the vehicle, maintaining it, and loading and unloading the goods are not necessarily parts of the exercise of the responsibility for the operation of the vehicle.

(2) Which partner is, in fact, responsible for carrying out that work?

(3) Does that partner hold a Certificate of Competence and does he or she have the time, capability and necessary commitment to carry out that work in a satisfactory way?'

'Full-time employment'

If a licence-holder's professional competence is to be supplied by an employed transport manager (which in the case of a company it can only be), he must be employed *full-time* by the licence-holder, under the definition of 'transport manager' in the regulations. This requirement has caused considerable difficulty, especially to owner-drivers or small operators not themselves qualified, and who cannot easily afford to employ a transport manager. The concept of 'full-time' employment does not appear in the EEC Directive, which merely requires that the person concerned 'will continuously and effectively manage the transport operations of the undertaking'. In Appeal 1979 No Q4 *Scotflow Limited* the Transport Tribunal had to deal with the argument that the introduction of the concept of full-time employment into the United Kingdom regulations was outside the powers conferred by the Directive. In their decision the Tribunal stated as follows: 'The real question is whether Regulation 5(1)(c) read with the definition of "transport manager" in Regulation 2(1) is *ultra vires*. Since Regulation 5(1)(c) is a method of achieving the result sought by the Directive of having the appellants transport operations continuously and effectively managed by a professionally competent person, and the Secretary of State is given by Art. 189 of the Treaty of Rome a choice of methods, we have come to the conclusion that Regulation 5(1)(c) is *intra vires* notwithstanding that it might also have included some other method of achieving the same result.'[20]

---

[20] The corresponding rules for Public Service Vehicle Operator Licences do not require the Transport Manager to be employed full time, although the EEC Directive relating to the entry into the profession of passenger transport is analogous with that for goods: Public Passenger Vehicles Act 1981, Schedule 3 para 4.

The meaning of 'full-time employment', assuming it to be *intra vires* (within the scope of the directive), was also questioned in the same case, it being suggested that it could mean employment for as many hours a week as are required to perform the duties – which in case of only one or two vehicles would be comparatively few. However, the Tribunal held that full-time employment meant employment during the whole of ordinary reasonable working hours. ('Reasonable' here presumably means 'customary'.) It follows that the same person cannot be the employed transport manager of more than one licence-holder. Problems may still arise where, for instance, two closely associated companies operate from the same premises, and the transport manager proposed for each company is a director of both and in fact responsible for the operations. The law is clear, but for a Licensing Authority exercising an administrative function the practical answer may be less so. It may be added that the insistence of Licence Authorities on genuine full-time employment has no doubt had the result of making many small operators qualify themselves by examination.

More than one transport manager

The power of the Licensing Authority to require more than one transport manager arose, under the 1977 Regulations, if the operator had more than one operating centre. The 1984 Regulations removed the power by repealing the 1977 Regulations and providing in paragraphs 3 and 4 of Schedule 6 that a company would satisfy the requirement as to professional competence by having *a* transport manager who is of good repute and professionally competent. The definition of 'transport manager' was amended by the substitution of the expression '. . . has continuous and effective responsibility for the management of the transport operations of the business' (following the language of the EEC Directive) for the earlier version '. . . and is in a position where he is responsible for the operation of vehicles used under the licence'.

The Goods Vehicles (Operators' Licences, Qualifications and Fees)(Amendment) Regulations 1986 SI No 666 amended Schedule 6 of the 1984 Regulations by (in effect) adding to paragraph 3 the words 'or such number of them as the Licensing Authority may require', after the words 'a transport manager', thus restoring the power to require more than one in relation to transport managers employed by companies. It did not, however, make the exercise of the power dependent on the operator's having more than one operating centre.

It will be relevant to consider some of the decisions of the Transport Tribunal about transport managers made while the 1977 Regulations were in force, in so far as they may still be applicable. In Appeal 1978 No P13 *Scot Bowyer Limited* the Tribunal decided that it was not a ground for refusing to grant a standard licence that the proposed transport manager would not be resident in the Traffic Area concerned, where there would be six depots or operating centres. The decision turned partly on the meaning of the words 'in a position where he is responsible . . .' in the 1977 definition of 'transport manager'. The Tribunal held that the words 'in a position' did not relate to geographical location, but to the nature of the employment; and so, provided that the individual in question was able continuously and effectively to manage the operations from his station outside the Traffic Area – as the Licensing Authority himself found he was – the applicants could not be compelled to have a transport manager resident in the Traffic Area. It is suggested that the same result would be reached under the 1984 Regulations – more so perhaps because of the disappearance of the ambiguous expression 'in a position'. The result would no doubt have been (and would still be) different if there were evidence that the transport manager could *not* 'continuously and effectively manage' the operations from his station outside the Traffic Area. If he could not do so he would not qualify as a transport manager at all in respect of the licence being applied for. The further the transport manager is from the scene of the operations, the heavier will be the burden of establishing continuous and effective management there.

There is now no guidance as to the circumstances in which a Licensing Authority can require an operator to have more than one transport manager. The formula in Schedule 6 of the 1984 Regulations as amended does not, for instance, contain any such expression as 'reasonably' or 'for good cause' – although of course any discretionary powers must be exercised reasonably. A Licensing Authority can give rulings and impose conditions only in respect of licences granted in his own Traffic Area; thus the Licensing Authority for the West Midlands Traffic Area (for example) could not, it is suggested, require a second transport manager to be employed in, say, Manchester, in order to provide more effective management at an operating centre in Birmingham, although if that were the proposal made to him by the applicant, he could accept it as satisfying the requirement (as in *Scot Bowyer*). He could, however, require more than one transport manager to be employed by a company to manage operations at one or more operating centres in the West Midlands Traffic Area. It should be remembered that the power to require more than one transport manager is exercisable in respect of companies only, and not individual licence-holders or partnerships.

Companies not infrequently supply with their application the names of two or more holders of Certificates of Professional Competence, with the intention that they should all be listed as 'Transport Managers' on the licence, whether or not there is more than one operating centre. No doubt the names often find their way onto licences; nevertheless the practice is strictly incorrect. The obligation, where it arises, is to have one transport manager with responsibility for the operations, unless the Licensing Authority (in the case of companies only) requires more than one. Of course the operator will have his own organisation, with foremen and managers in charge of various parts of the operation; some or all may hold Certificates of Professional Competence. Only one of these (exceptionally more if required by the Licensing Authority) will be *the* transport manager.[21] It will be a required condition of the licence, under Regulation 7(1) of the 1984 Regulations, that any change in the identity or continued employment of the transport manager shall be notified to the Licensing Authority within 28 days. In Appeal 1978 No P12 *William Press & Son Ltd* the Transport Tribunal indicated that the cessation of employment of *any* named individual might be made the subject of a condition under section 66 of the 1968 Act[22] if the Licensing Authority so determined, but not primarily in the capacity of transport manager; the statutory condition must relate to the transport manager proposed by the applicant, accepted as being professionally competent and of good repute by the Licensing Authority, and named in the licence.

The consequences of an operator ceasing to have professional competence because of the death, resignation etc of his transport manager, are dealt with in Chapter 7.

---

[21] See Appeal 1978 No P12 *William Press & Son Ltd* for a discussion of the distinction between 'the transport manager' and other persons employed in management positions.
[22] Conditions under section 66 are dealt with on pp 84 – 5.

CHAPTER 3

Objections and Representations

This subject will be dealt with in two sections, the first covering objections under section 63(3) of the 1968 Act, on the grounds that one or more of the requirements of section 64(2) will not be met by the applicant; the second covering the field of objections and representations on environmental grounds under the provisions of section 52 and Schedule 4 of the Transport Act 1982, amending and adding to those of the 1968 Act. The two fields are mutually exclusive in relation to their subject matter, although a 'statutory objector' may join an objection made under section 63(3) with one under section 69B, provided that it is made clear whether they are objecting under section 63 or section 69 or both, and their objections are particularised under the appropriate section.[1]

Objections under section 63

Section 63(3) and Regulation 13(1) of the 1984 Regulations require the Licensing Authority to publish in *Applications and Decisions*[2] notice of every application for an operator's licence received by him, and section 68(4) extends that requirement to most variation applications. Section 63(3) provides that certain persons and bodies (referred to here as 'statutory objectors') may within the period prescribed by the regulations – 21 days from the date of publication in *A & D* – object to the grant of any application for a licence or variation so published.

---

[1] Appeal 1985 No W30 *Strathkelvin District Council* v. *Fife Forwarding Company Limited.*
[2] Usually referred to as *A & D*; this is the publication in which the Licensing Authority publishes notices of applications, hearings etc as required by section 63(1).

They are:

- (a) a prescribed trade union or association; [3]
- (b) a chief officer of police;
- (c) a local authority, ie a regional county or district council;
- (d) a planning authority. [4]

Objection may be made on the ground that any of the requirements mentioned in section 64(2) are not satisfied in the case of the application. Section 63(3) has not been amended to add a reference to the requirements of the 1977 Qualification Regulations or the 1984 Regulations which replaced them, namely as to the good repute, financial standing or professional competence of the applicant for a standard licence. However, the 1977 Operators' Licences Regulations (SI 1977 No 1737) required, by Regulation 9, that every objection should be in a form set out in Schedule 2, paragraphs (f) and (g) of which related to standard licences and referred, respectively, to financial resources and professional competence. There was no paragraph relating to good repute. The 1984 Regulations reproduced Regulation 9 (as Regulation 17) without reference to a schedule, which indeed did not reappear. It is therefore speciously arguable (on the grounds of *vires*) that no right of objection now subsists on any of the three 'EEC' grounds; and somewhat more solidly, that no objection can (or ever could) be properly instituted on the ground of good repute. In practice objections are lodged on grounds of 'no good repute', and so far as the writer is aware have not been challenged otherwise than on the merits.

There is no provision for any persons or bodies other than the statutory objectors to object to or make representations about an application on other than environmental grounds. It is however not unheard of for other persons to try to lodge representations and to seek to be heard at an inquiry. Often these will be creditors of the applicant claiming that his failure to meet his financial obligations casts doubt on his financial standing or indeed his fitness or good repute; occasionally a police officer will offer information about an applicant's record, although his Chief Constable has not formally objected. The Transport Tribunal in Appeal 1983 No U10 *L & P Traffic Services Ltd* gave guidance on the procedure to be adopted in such cases. They ruled that a solicitor purporting to appear for a non-

---

[3] Those prescribed by regulation 17(2) are: The British Association of Removers, The Freight Transport Association, The General and Municipal Workers Union, The Road Haulage Association, The Transport and General Workers' Union, The Union of Shop, Distributive and Allied Workers, The United Road Transport Union.

[4] Added by the Transport Act 1982.

statutory representor should not be permitted to cross-examine the applicant or his witnesses, or make submissions, nor may letters written by or on behalf of such a representor be received in evidence; however, if the Licensing Authority knows that a person has material evidence to give bearing directly on one of the relevant requirements, he is entitled to call such a witness himself. They added that such occasions would be rare and said: 'An example is the calling of a police officer to give evidence as to the circumstances of a conviction or convictions to help the Licensing Authority on the issues of fitness and repute. An applicant, however, should be given the earliest possible notification of the Licensing Authority's intention to call such a witness together with the substance of his evidence.'

A statutory objector who, having duly made an objection to an application for the grant or variation of a licence, is aggrieved by the grant of it has a right of appeal to the Transport Tribunal under section 70 of the 1968 Act.[5]

Environmental objections and representations under section 69B

The Transport Act 1982 contained a series of provisions intended to supply the deficiency identified by *Cash and McCall*,[6] namely to give to Licensing Authorities a measure of control over operating centres on environmental grounds. Section 52 of the Act, under the heading 'environmental control of goods vehicle operating centres' and side-lined in similar terms, provided as follows:

'(1) The operating centre of any authorised vehicle under a goods vehicle operator's licence granted under Part V of the Transport Act 1968 shall be the base or centre at which it is normally kept (whether or not it is also used from there) . . .'

and the definition in section 92(1) of the 1968 Act was amended accordingly.[7] Subsection (2) provided that the provisions set out in Part I of Schedule 4 should be inserted in Part V of the 1968 Act immediately after section 69. They are numbered 69A to 69G, and each will be considered separately. The provisions of section 52 and Schedule 4 came into force on 1 June 1984, and therefore applied to applications made on or after that date. Applications received before

---

[5] See Chapter 9, for appeal rights and procedures.
[6] Appeal 1975 No M15 *RHA Ltd* v. *A Cash and McCall*.
[7] Of course this is now the definition for all purposes, and not only in the context of environmental control.

that date were not affected, notwithstanding that the resulting licences issued may have been dated after 1 June. Transitional provisions dealt with the conversion of old-style operating centres, as defined in the original section 92(1) and interpreted according to *Cash & McCall*, into the new-style ones based on where the vehicles are normally kept.[8] It needs to be borne in mind that for a period of up to five years from 1 June 1984 there will be licences in existence, diminishing in number month by month as they expire and are 'renewed' under the new rules, which were not subject to objection on environmental grounds and which do not have 'approved' operating centres specified.

Before embarking on an analysis of the provisions it is perhaps relevant to refer to the considered opinion of the Transport Tribunal on the environmental legislation as a whole, if only to illustrate the risks inherent in offering opinions as to its interpretation. In Appeal 1985 No W17 *Surrey Heath Borough Council* v. *NFT Distribution Ltd* the Tribunal referred to the 'tortuous and unfortunately drafted provisions of this Act', and added a little further on: 'the environmental provisions of this Act are unhappily drafted.' It is perhaps significant that of the 55 appeals decided after full hearing in 1985, 1986 and 1987, 36 were concerned with questions arising out of the new environmental provisions.

The legislative framework

There are three central provisions for environmental control of operating centres, effective in relation to applications made on or after 1 June 1984:

   (i)   a person may not use a place in the area of any Licensing Authority as an operating centre for authorised vehicles under any operator's licence granted to him by that authority unless it is specified in that licence: section 69A(1); section 69A(4) makes breach of this subsection an offence punishable by a fine up to £500. In addition, section 69F(2) provides that contravention of section 69A(1) will make the licence subject to revocation, suspension, premature termination or curtailment by the Licensing Authority under the powers conferred by section 69(1).[9]

---

[8]   The Transport Act (Commencement No 5) Order 1984 SI 1984 No 175 provided that in respect of any licence then in force, as from 1 June 1984 the place which was the actual operating centre under section 52 (ie the place where the vehicles were normally kept) was deemed to be the specified operating centre under the licence. This might be the same or a different place, depending on circumstances.

[9]   For section 69(1) see Table of Statutes, p 157.

(ii) every application for the grant or variation of a licence (other than a 'trivial' variation [10]) must be advertised in a local newspaper circulating in each locality affected by the application, ie where the proposed operating centre is situated: section 69E;

(iii) a statutory objector may object on the ground that the operating centre is unsuitable on environmental grounds for use as such; section 69B(1); and any owner or occupier of land in the vicinity of the operating centre may, subject to certain conditions,[11] make representations against a grant on the same grounds: section 69B(2).

Sections 69A and 69E

Every applicant for an operator's licence (including a 'renewal') must state in his application each place in the area of the Licensing Authority which will be an operating centre if the licence is granted. The application will of course be published in *A & D* in the usual way, but in addition the applicant must insert a notice in a local newspaper circulating in the locality of the operating centre within 21 days either side of the date on which the application is lodged. Section 69E requires the Licensing Authority to refuse the application without considering its merits unless he is satisfied that this has been duly done. Schedule 3 to the 1984 Regulations, SI 1984 No 176, prescribed a skeleton text for this notice, but the amending regulations operative from 1 May 1986 (SI 1986 No 666) substituted a new schedule merely listing the matters to be included, and requiring specific wording only in relation to the rights of owners and occupiers of land to make representations. The prescribed wording is as follows:

'Owners or occupiers of land (including buildings) in the vicinity of the operating centre or centres who believe the use or enjoyment of the land will be prejudicially affected, may make written representations to the Licensing Authority at [address of Traffic Area Office] within the 21 days following the publication of this notice. Representors must at the same time send a copy of their representations to the applicant at the address given in this notice.'

The application form GV79 asks the applicant to state when and where the notice has been or will be published, or (as is usually done) to enclose the original notice as it appeared, showing the name of the

---

[10] See p 44, 82 – 3.
[11] As set out in detail on p 49 below.

paper and the date. An advertisement which is out of time, or omits any essential element, eg the address or description of the proposed operating centre(s) or the number of vehicles and trailers to be kept there, will be rejected as not complying with section 69E, with summary refusal of the application to follow.[12]

Some elements of these sections need to be separately examined.

Operating centre and 'normally kept'

The test is whether the vehicles will be 'normally kept' at the designated place. This expression is not defined in the Act or Regulations, and has not been interpreted by the Transport Tribunal except in a negative way. In Appeal 1985 No W12 *J Cryer & Sons Ltd* they said: 'There was no evidence that any of the vehicles were "normally kept" anywhere other than at the Paragon Industrial Estate. Occasional use, even on a regular basis, of another place to park a vehicle overnight will not render that place the vehicle's operating centre if it is *normally* kept elsewhere.' [The Tribunal's underlining.] In the context of the appeal, this dictum was incidental and it leaves unanswered the question of what 'normally kept' does mean. Complaints from members of the public that an operator is regularly parking his vehicles in their street or outside their houses are frequently received by Licensing Authorities, with requests for enforcement action to be taken. Whatever the view of the Transport Tribunal, it is by no means certain that magistrates would take the same view as to whether there was not here an unauthorised operating centre.

Difficult questions arise in cases where the nature of the operation is such that the vehicles are perpatetic and have no regular base; or where the operator hires the vehicles from different sources and does not 'keep' them anywhere. It is clear that every operator must have an operating centre, as without one he cannot apply to any Licensing Authority for a licence,[13] nor can he comply with section 69A(1). It is suggested that an operator faced with this problem can only name as his operating centre the place with which his vehicles have some 'normal' connection, however tenuous.

---

[12] Where the advertisement is dated more than 21 days *after* the application, most licensing authorities allow the application to be redated to a later date to avoid the need for a fresh application to be made, provided that in renewal cases the new date is still earlier than the date of expiry of the previous licence so that continuity is preserved – see p 46.

[13] By reason of section 62(1): see p 45, and Appeal 1987 No Y12 *Mid Suffolk District Council* v. *Dowell Junior (trading as A Dowell & Sons (Bury))*.

Local newspaper circulating in the locality

'Local newspaper' presumably includes free newspapers which are delivered to some or all houses, whether requested or not. It is open to question whether it would include newspapers in languages other than English, perhaps if the locality contained a substantial number of speakers of such languages.

It is sometimes alleged by would-be representors after a licence has been granted that they did not see the advertisement because the newspaper chosen by the applicant does not 'circulate' in the locality. It is in practice impossible for the Licensing Authority's staff to know at application stage whether the newspaper in which the advertisement was placed does or does not circulate in the locality. The term 'circulate' used of newspapers has no precise legal meaning; the *Oxford English Dictionary* defines it, in the context, as 'to pass into the hands of readers, to be extensively taken and read'. Each case would have to be considered on its merits, with such principles in mind. If the question is raised before the grant of the licence, eg by a statutory objector, or even by a representor who has seen the advertisement by chance, the Licensing Authority will have to determine first of all whether or not the provisions of section 69E require him to refuse the application out of hand. If the question is raised after the grant of the licence, and it were shown, by whatever criteria judged, that the newspaper concerned did not circulate in the locality, would the grant be void, or voidable, or wholly beyond recall? If section 69E goes to jurisdiction, so that the Licensing Authority had no power to entertain the application, the grant would be void from the outset; however the test is whether the Licensing Authority was 'satisfied', and on these supposed facts he *was* satisfied on *prima facie* evidence which, as it turned out, should not have satisfied him. In the absence of a decided case, the suggestion is tentatively put forward that the discovery that the newspaper did not circulate in the locality could be treated as a material change of circumstances under section 69(1)(e) with a view to revocation (or perhaps premature termination) and a fresh application. (see p 106 for discussion of section 69(1)(e).)

'Objectors and representors'

It will be convenient to keep the two terms distinct, the former being confined to the 'statutory' persons and bodies entitled by sections 63 and 69B(1) to object to applications, the latter being owners and occupiers of land given the right under section 69B(2) to make representations about them. The question has nevertheless sometimes been raised, whether a statutory objector can properly make representations, eg where a local authority officer may have seen the newspaper advertisement before publication of the application in *A & D*. In Appeal 1985 No W30 *Strathkelvin District Council* v. *Fife Forwarding Company Ltd* the Council had written to the Licensing Authority raising certain points in oppostion to the application, and referring to them as 'representations'. The notice was received more than 21 days after the advertisement, but was 'in time' in relation to the publication in *Applications and Decisions*, although the Council did not formally object by reference to that publication. The applicants argued that the Council's points could be treated only as 'representations' and as such were out of time; they therefore had no right to be heard as appellants. The Tribunal dismissed this argument and said: 'It was quite clear that the Appellants [ie the Council] were making objection under either section 69B(1) or section 63 of the Transport Act 1968. The appellants' use of the word "representations", however, was unfortunate having regard to the distinction drawn in the Act between objections and representations, and local authorities should be careful to use appropriate terminology.'

The grounds for an objection or representation under either section 69B(1) or (2) is that 'any place which, if the licence is granted, will be an operating centre of the holder of the licence is unsuitable on environmental grounds for use as such'. However, while the rights of representors under section 69B(2) are subject to certain requirements as to ownership or occupation of land in the vicinity, and as to the likelihood of the use or enjoyment of their property being prejudicially affected (see further, on p 48), the statutory objectors have only to establish unsuitability on environmental grounds, and for this purpose they may call as witnesses persons who may not qualify as representors under section 69B(2).[14] In particular, as will be seen (pp 48 and 77), a local authority objecting under section 69B(1) is not limited to the narrow definition of 'vicinity' which restricts the class of representors entitled to make a case under section 69B(2).

While it is a feature of the legislation that neither the word 'environmental' nor the expression 'on environmental grounds' is anywhere defined or explained, section 69G(1) requires any objection or representation to contain 'particulars of any matters alleged by the person making the objection or representations to be relevant to the determination of the Licensing Authority . . .'. The matters relevant to such determinations are prescribed, under a power in section 69G(3), in Regulation 22 of the 1984 Regulations under eight

---

[14] See, for instance, Appeal 1987 No Y12 *Mid Suffolk District Council* v. *A Dowell Junior*.

paragraphs (a) to (h). These will be dealt with in detail later (see pp 77 ff), but it is relevant to draw attention, in this context, to Regulation 22(1)(a), which refers to any effect which the use of the land as an operating centre has or would be likely to have on the environment of the vicinity of that land. This expression entitles an objecting local authority to look to a wider 'vicinity' than that limiting the locus of representors under section 69B(2).[15]

It is fair to say that the matters of which particulars must be given in any objection or representation, by virtue of this regulation, are not themselves matters of environmental complaint, but rather aspects of the planning position and the various factors which might or might not form the background to the situation.[16] It is presumably not unreasonable to assume that Licensing Authorities will take judicial notice of what 'adverse effects on environmental conditions' are likely to be caused by; and certainly despite section 69G and Regulation 22, representors do usually give details of the actual matters complained of, which by and large may be comprehended by the term 'actionable nuisance', ie noise, fumes, dust, visual intrusion, etc.

Representations

The persons given the right to make representations against the grant of an application for a licence or a variation of a licence on environmental grounds are owners or occupiers of land in the vicinity of the operating centre. The right to do so is subject to the proviso that any adverse effects on environmental conditions arising from the use of the operating centre as such would be capable of prejudicially affecting the use or enjoyment of the land.[17]

'Owner' is defined, by an amendment to section 92(1) of the 1968 Act made by paragraph 7 of Part II of Schedule 4 to the 1982 Act, in the following terms:

> ' "owner", in relation to any land in England and Wales, means a person, other than a mortgagee not in possession, who, whether in his own right or as trustee for any other person, is entitled to receive the rack rent of the land, or, where the land is not let at a rack rent, would be so entitled if it were so let.'

---

[15] Appeal 1986 No X25 *Surrey County Council and Surrey Heath Borough Council* v. *Rupert William Carter and Nicholas David Carter (t/a CC Express Hay and Straw Services).*

[16] eg the number and type of vehicles, times when they will be in use, nature and frequency of ingress and egress etc.

[17] Representors cannot complain about inconvenience in using the public highway itself, if no nuisance is felt within their property: Appeal 1987 No Y28 *P T Chesney (t/a C & H Carriers).*

'Occupier' is not defined, but presumably includes any actual occupier, including a tenant at will, licensee, squatter or even trespasser. The scope of the concept of 'occupier' is, however, limited by the proviso referred to above, which it will be observed is a condition precedent to the right of the owner or occupier to make a representation at all. There must be at least the possibility that the use or enjoyment of the land would be affected. Although the language used would extend to 'the use or enjoyment' generally, ie by any person who might at any time occupy the land, the primary intention of the provision is presumably to relate the use or enjoyment to the actual owner or occupier who makes the representation. However, it is suggested that an absentee owner of an unoccupied property could make a valid representation on the ground that the use or enjoyment of the property by a hypothetical tenant or licensee would be capable of being prejudicially affected. Certainly it is not uncommon for a Parish Council to make a representation on the strength of its ownership of the village green, [18] the use or enjoyment of which by the parishioners could be prejudicially affected. Questions may also arise as to who is the occupier of, say, a school or a church for the purposes of the section; no more can be said than that each case must be treated on its merits.

The Transport Tribunal has ruled that a Residents' Association, which does not own land, cannot make a representation, [19] although of course those members of it who resided in the vicinity could do so, and under the terms of Regulation 23(2) could be represented at the inquiry, at the Licensing Authority's discretion, by an officer of the Association.

'In the vicinity'

This expression is nowhere defined, and it is used in the Act and Regulations in other contexts in which it may not necessarily have the same meaning as in sections 69B(2) and 69D(5) (see footnote [15] on p 48). Regarding the proviso about the effect on the use or enjoyment of the land, it seems reasonable to suppose that 'in the vicinity' must mean near enough for such effects arising from the use of the operating centre to amount to a nuisance to the owners or occupiers. In Appeal 1985 No W17 *Surrey Heath Borough Council* v. *NFT Distribution Ltd* the Transport Tribunal had to consider whether the Licensing Authority had been justified in defining the vicinity by

---

[18] In one case it owned 'part of the village pond': Appeal 1985 No W4 *R A Nightingale t/a Anglia Fruiterers.*

[19] Appeals 1984 No V22 *UK Corrugated Ltd* and 1985 No W11 *R G Brimley (t/a Retailset).*

reference to particular distances from the operating centre, and declining to take into account representations from persons owning or occupying land beyond those limits. They said: 'It is for each Licensing Authority to decide in relation to each case what is within the vicinity of the operating centre. This will be different in different locations. The Licensing Authority may well consider that a relevant factor is whether adverse environmental effects which emerge from that centre are likely to be heard or otherwise felt in this or that position.' This may be conveniently referred to as the 'earshot test'.[20]

In the *NFT* case, as in many such cases, a major ground of complaint and representation was that the applicant's vehicles do or will cause damage and/or disturbance to the occupiers of houses fronting on roads in the area who do not hear or feel effects emerging from the centre itself. They claim, however, to be in the vicinity in the general sense, and argue that the prejudicial effects which they suffer are due to the vehicles being kept where they are and going to and from that place, and therefore arise from the use of the operating centre as such. The Tribunal, in the *NFT* case, said as to this: 'In our judgment noise or vibration from authorised vehicles on approach roads to the operating centre are not relevant to the determination of the extent of the vicinity under the Act or Regulations.'[21]

Note: This statement must now be read subject to a dictum of the Tribunal in the *Hay & Straw Services* case. The Tribunal, having said that the question did not arise for decision in the case, proceeded to 'deal with it' in the following terms: 'It does seem that the Licensing Authority understood the Tribunal to have said [in the *NFT* case] that a place could not be within the vicinity of an operating centre if people at that point could not hear or feel adverse environmental effects emerging from the operating centre itself. In so holding he misdirected himself. In determining what lies within the vicinity of an operating centre a Licensing Authority is considering what is physically related to or near to the operating centre. Whether adverse environmental effects emerging from the centre itself can be heard or felt at this or that point is only one of the factors which he may take into account in that determination. If the Licensing Authority had not misdirected himself in this way it seem probable that he would have found that all the houses bordering on or close to the private road were within the vicinity of the operating centre.'

---

[20] This test does not apply to cases where a local authority objects under section 69B(1) – see Appeal cited in the preceding note.

[21] See also Appeal 1986 No X30 *W R Atkinson (Transport) Ltd,* discussed on pp 53, 90.

It is relevant to note that in the *Hay & Straw* case:

(i)   no person claiming to be 'in the vicinity' of the operating centre made a representation under section 69B(2);

(ii)   the question of the interpretation of the words in that section was therefore not before the Licensing Authority;

(iii)   the Tribunal emphasised that it was only *'when considering objections under section 69B(1)'* that a Licensing Authority should have regard to the environmental effects of vehicles going to and from the operating centre.

Since the Tribunal emphasised the non-binding nature of their dictum, it would perhaps be premature to speculate on the meaning to be attributed to 'what is physically related to or near to the operating centre'. However interpreted, 'vicinity' in section 69B(2) is a test of legal standing (*locus*) only, whereas in regulation 22(1)(a), (b) and (c) it defines the scope of the Licensing Authority's consideration of the merits of the environmental issue.

The Tribunal in the *NFT* case considered whether, having determined the vicinity in accordance with the 'earshot test', effects arising from vehicles moving on roads within that vicinity could be the subject of representations. They did not arrive at a final answer to this question, but their consideration of it brought them close, it is suggested, to an affirmative answer. They pointed out that under section 69B(3) an application could be refused if the *parking* of the authorised vehicles in the vicinity of the operating centre would cause adverse environmental effects, and asked why other activities of authorised vehicles within the vicinity – eg moving, or waiting with engines running – should not also be a proper subject for representations. It is suggested with some confidence that a Licensing Authority who accepted and acted on representations in such circumstances would not be lightly reversed on that ground on appeal.

It is a common complaint in representations that the grant of the application in question will or may give rise to road safety hazards, especially in relation to children, and the opportunity is taken by representors to raise issues of highway suitability, speed limits, standards of driving, etc. As has already been noted, these are not considered to be matters falling within the scope of 'environmental' representations, although they would be proper grounds for objection by statutory objectors under section 63(3).

Procedures for objection and representation

The procedures for making objections and representations are prescribed by Regulations 18 and 19 of the 1984 Regulations, as amended by the Goods Vehicle (Operators' Licences, Qualifications and Fees) (Amendment) Regulations 1986, SI 1986 No 666, and further by Regulations with the same title made in 1987, SI 1987 No 841. These Regulations are as follows:

18.   The prescribed manner in which an objection or a representation about an application shall be made is that it shall:

(a)   be written;

(b)   be signed:

  (i)   if made by an individual, by that person;

  (ii)   if made by persons in partnership, by all of the partners or by one of them with the authority of the others;

  (iii)   if made by any other body or group of persons, by one or more individual persons authorised for that purpose by the body or group;

or, in any of the above cases, by a solicitor acting on behalf of (as the case may be) the person, body or group; and

(c)   state the grounds on which it is made.

A copy of every objection or representation shall be sent by the objector, or the person making the representation, to the applicant at the same time as it is sent to the Licensing Authority.

19.   (1) An objection to an application shall be made so as to be received by the Licensing Authority not later than 21 days from the date on which notice of the application is published in *Applications and Decisions*.

(2) A representation in respect of an application shall be made so as to be received by the Licensing Authority within 21 days from the date on which notice of the application is published as required by regulation 13(2).[22]

In both paragraphs 19(1) and 19(2) the 1984 regulatons had 'within 21 days'; the 1986 amendment altered 'within' to 'not later than' in 19(1) but not in 19(2). The significance of the distinction is not apparent.

Regulation 20 allows the Licensing Authority 'in circumstances which he considers to be exceptional' to consider any objection or representation, notwithstanding that all or any of the requirements

---

[22] ie in a local newspaper.

specified in Regulations 18 and 19(1) or (2), as the case may be, are not complied with. This provision is to be narrowly interpreted: in Appeal 1984 No V21 *Auto Industries Ltd* the Tribunal said 'Lack of objection by an applicant does not of itself justify a Licensing Authority in hearing representations from a person who has not complied with Regulations 18 and 19 . . . ''exceptional'' is a strong word. Unless there are circumstances which the Licensing Authority considers exceptional, a person who has not complied with Regulations 18 and 19 cannot make representations, even when no objection is taken by the applicant.' The Tribunal in Appeal 1984 No V22 *UK Corrugated* added this general warning: 'It is very important that the Regulations are strictly complied with. They are in our judgment drawn in a way designed to prevent a Public Inquiry becoming a kind of general meeting at which any resident who wishes to have a say is permitted to do so.' However, provided the Licensing Authority directs himself correctly and makes no error in law, his decision as to whether exceptional circumstances exist or not will not normally be interfered with. Thus in Appeal 1986 No X30 *W R Atkinson (Transport) Ltd* the Tribunal rejected a submission that exceptional circumstances should not have been found, saying ' . . . the appellants cannot succeed unless they can show that no reasonable licensing authority could properly have concluded on the evidence that special (sic) circumstances existed.'

The decisions of Licensing Authorities not to accept objections from local authorities on grounds of their being out of time or failing to copy to the applicant have been upheld in Appeals 1985 No W16 *Canterbury City Council* v. *BRS Southern* and 1985 No W17 *Surrey Heath Borough Council* v. *NFT Distribution Ltd* (in which Surrey Heath were *not* the Council in default). In the latter case the Tribunal observed that a Licensing Authority will rightly set a severer standard in the case of statutory objectors than in the case of private representors, who do not have the same ready access to legal advice.

Consideration of objections and representations

Section 64(1) of the Act provides that in considering an application for an operator's licence the Licensing Authority 'shall have regard to any objection duly made under Section 63'. The available grounds of objection under this section have already been discussed (pp 40 – 42); it is relevant to note that although statutory objectors may object under section 69B(1) by virtue of their right to do so under section 63, they do not in so doing object 'under' section 63, which confines the grounds of objection to the requirements of section

64(2). The 1982 Act did not aim to amend section 63 or section 64 in this regard, but provided by section 69G(4) that in making any determination about the suitability of any place on environmental grounds the Licensing Authority shall have regard to any objections or representations duly made under sections 69B or 69D. The Licensing Authority will, it is assumed, accept as 'duly made' any objection which complies with Regulations 18 and 19, and if it is not withdrawn or compromised, will almost certainly consider it at a Public Inquiry. Representations, on the other hand, will be more closely scrutinised, because in addition to the requirements of Regulations 18 and 19, the representors must also satisfy the licensing authority, *prima facie* at least, (a) that they own or occupy property; (b) that this property is in the vicinity of the operating centre; and (c) their use or enjoyment of this property is capable of being prejudicially affected. Failure to fulfil any of these conditions will disqualify a representor. The one most likely to be found wanting is that relating to vicinity, which the Licensing Authority or his staff may be able to judge from maps or plans available to them or supplied by one or other of the parties. If an application has attracted an objection from a local authority as well as representations, the Licensing Authority may suggest to unqualified or doubtfully qualified representors that they should offer themselves as witnesses to be called by the objecting Council.

Representors, whether in the vicinity or not, very often base their representations on general amenity or planning grounds, such as that the area is one of outstanding natural beauty, or is in the Green Belt, or that the applicant has not got planning permission for what he proposes. These are by themselves not valid grounds for representations, and the representors will probably be advised by the Licensing Authority's staff to approach their local District, Borough or County Council with a view to their lodging an objection. The would-be representors could then be called as witnesses by the statutory objector. A representor has no right of appeal from any decision of the Licensing Authority, but the Transport Tribunal Rules 1986, SI 1986 No 1547, now provide that representors are to be informed if an appeal has been lodged, and will have the right to apply to the Transport Tribunal for leave to become parties to the appeal. Any person given leave to become a party will have a right to be heard. (For further discussion of these rules see pp 127 – 28.)

The lack of a right of appeal for representors reinforces the need for their representations to be fully and fairly considered, and not excluded from consideration on other than grounds fully established under the Regulations. In Appeal 1986 No X34 *R G and M T Jury (t/a R & G Transport)* v. *Devon County Council* the Tribunal pointed out that the duty of determining finally whether the grounds on which a representation is made are good or bad falls upon the Licensing Authority (or his Deputy) personally. His staff may well, under appropriate directives or guidance, 'sieve' letters of representation and reject those which clearly do not meet the requirements of the Regulations in some particular. However, they suggested that the effect of Regulations 18, 19 and 20 of the 1984 Regulations SI 176 is that, provided that a representation about an application is written, signed by the representor or his solicitor, states the grounds on which it is made and is in time and copied to the applicant, the Licensing Authority himself is required under Regulation 20(3) to consider the representation in deciding whether or not to hold an inquiry and/or grant the application.

Decisions in 'environmental' cases

Where objections or representations have been made against an application under sections 69B(1) or (2), with or without objections under section 63, the Licensing Authority will have to consider the requirements of section 64, as he is required to do in every case.[23] If these requirements are met, having regard to any objections under section 63, the application will normally be granted, subject to any limitations imposed under section 64(4) or conditions under section 66.[24] Only if an objection or representation is 'duly made' under section 69B(1) or (2) may he refuse an application on environmental grounds. If such an objection or representation has been made, the options open to the Licensing Authority in deciding the case – in addition to simply granting the application – are set out in sections 69B(3) to (6).

Section 69B(3) provides that he may in any such case refuse an application on the ground that the parking of authorised vehicles at or in the vicinity of any operating centre applied for would cause adverse effects on environmental conditions in its vicinity. The significance of this provision is further considered in a note on parking on p 75.

Section 69B(4) provides that, subject to subsection (5) relating to material change (see following paragraph), he may refuse the application on the ground that any proposed operating centre is unsuitable for use as such on environmental grounds other than that of parking mentioned in subsection (3).

---

[23] By section 64(1), see p 14.
[24] Conditions under section 66 are dealt with on pp 84-91.

Section 69B(5) provides that the Licensing Authority may *not* refuse an application on environmental grounds if the applicant satisfies him that the grant of the application will not result in any material change as regards the places used or to be used as operating centres, or the use of any such place already in use under an existing licence. This provision requires further analysis, and is dealt with in detail in Chapter 5.

Section 69B(6) provides that the Licensing Authority may, in cases where more than one operating centre is proposed by the applicant under section 69A(2), grant the application limited to any operating centre or centres which is or are not unsuitable. By section 69B(7) an 'interim licence', if granted despite an objection or representation may specify such place or places nominated under section 69A(2) as the Authority thinks fit.

CHAPTER 4

Public Inquiries

Preliminaries

The Licensing Authority, under **section 87(1)** of the 1968 Act, may hold such inquiries as he thinks necessary for the proper exercise of his functions. He is not bound to do so except where he proposes to revoke, suspend, prematurely terminate or curtail a licence, or disqualify a licence-holder, and the licence-holder requests an inquiry: **section 69(9).**[1] Except in cases where he is precluded from granting a licence, eg if an applicant for a standard licence is not professionally competent, a Licensing Authority will not refuse a genuine application (whether objected to or not) without first hearing it at a Public Inquiry, at which the applicant will be called upon to satisfy him that the requirements of section 64(2) of the 1968 Act and, for standard licences, of the Qualification Regulations, are met. If an objection has been duly made, the application will normally be heard at a Public Inquiry,[2] at which the burden of proof of the facts on which the objection is based will lie on the objectors: **section 63(5).**

Similar considerations apply to representors under **section 69B(2)**, whose representations have been accepted as complying with the requirements of the section and the Regulations. If they comply with the requirements and are not withdrawn or compromised, the representors will usually be invited to present their case at a Public Inquiry, at which, as with objectors, the burden of proof rests upon them: **section 69G(1).**

Applications for licences or variations cannot be refused on environmental grounds unless an objection or representation has been duly made (see sections 69B(3) and (4) and section 69D(7)) but there is no requirement that objectors and representors should attend the inquiry. Indeed, as will be seen, representors may have their case presented by counsel, solicitors or other persons (see p 62); however,

---

[1] For Public Inquiries under section 69, see pp 93-108.
[2] A Licensing Authority may however reach a decision without a Public Inquiry even if an objection has been made: see Appeal 1986 No X27 *Wellingborough Borough Council & W Brown (Leather Goods),* discussed on p60.

as the burden of proof rests on them, and the facts on which they rely are likely to be peculiarly within their knowledge, a Licensing Authority is perhaps unlikely to refuse an application on environmental grounds if they, or at least one or more of them, do not attend. Experience has shown that, on average, only some 20 – 25% of representors who have lodged written representations choose to attend the inquiry. [3]

The essential requirement, in relation to any inquiry, is that the applicant should be fully informed of the case he has to meet. [4] In straightforward applications without objections or representations, the Licensing Authority will set out in the call-in letter the essential requirements of section 64(2) and will draw attention to any particular issues he proposes to inquire into: for instance if there is an issue as to good repute he will set out the convictions or other matters intended to be referred to in that connection. On the other hand, if it is self-evident that certain matters will be considered, particular reference to them will not be an essential element. In Appeal 1983 No U10 *L & P Traffic Services Ltd* the appellants submitted that the pro forma letter did not specifically state that their financial standing would be considered, although it had asked for accounts to be produced. The Tribunal observed: 'This request for information was a clear indication that section 64(2)(e) would probably be considered. Further, as already pointed out, the financial requirements under regulation 5 are more stringent than under section 64(2)(e) and the Licensing Authority has no discretion as to whether to take them into account. As should have been well known to the appellants and their advisers, the Licensing Authority must take them into account and be satisfied that they are fulfilled before granting a licence.'

Nevertheless the Tribunal are alert to the possiblity, in any sort of inquiry, that an unrepresented operator may not fully appreciate the possible consequences for his business of an adverse decision, and they have more than once [5] concluded a judgment with a recommendation that every 'call-in' letter in such a case should contain a statement that the operator should consider taking informed advice, eg from a solicitor. Indeed the extent of the duty to supply an applicant with particulars has perhaps widened in recent years. In a 1972 Appeal, No J17 *Witney Plant Hire & Haulage Co Ltd*, the Transport Tribunal said: 'In our view, there is no duty on the Licensing Authority to give particulars under this provision [sc.

---

[3]   This is a rough estimate; no figures have been published.
[4]   This topic will be fully explored in relation to 'disciplinary' inquiries in a later chapter, see p00.
[5]   Appeal 1982 No T11 *M Dyer & W H Cork (t/a M & B Transport)*;
      Appeal 1982 No V4 *D W Briggs (Plant Hire) Ltd*.

section 64(2)(d)] . . . Under section 64 proceedings are initiated by the applicant for a licence, and it is for him to satisfy the Licensing Authority positively concerning the various requirements set out in s.64(2): it is not for the Licensing Authority to form a *prima facie* view that one or more of the requirements is not satisfied and to give particulars of his reasons for that view.'

Where objections and/or representations have been duly made the applicant will be forewarned and presumably forearmed. It is of course essential that the objections should be clearly stated, with full particulars given. In Appeal 1983 No U20 *Road Haulage Association Ltd* v. *Kammac Trucking Ltd* the Transport Tribunal said: 'This notice of objection had been filled in in a very casual and unhelpful way. An allegation that a person or company is unfit by reason of his conduct to hold an operator's licence is a very serious allegation and proper particulars should always be given so that the applicant may understand each respect in which he is alleged to be unfit . . . and thus prepare as fully as possible to meet the objection.' It may be noted, in this connection, that there is now no prescribed form for objections or representations.

Response to objections and representations

Although there is no statutory requirement to that effect, an applicant for a licence in respect of whose application representations have been duly made under section 69B(2) is invited to give further particulars of his operation (on Form GV79E) and comment on the representations of which he has had copies. He is usually asked to list these, so that would-be representors who do not appear in the list can be eliminated as not having complied with Regulation 18, or invited to state the 'exceptional circumstances' under Regulation 20(4).[6] Under Regulation 16(1)(b) a representor, or a person authorised by him or her, has the right to inspect 'such part of the application as is, in the opinion of the licensing authority, relevant to the representation'. For this purpose the Licensing Authority may make the application (or part of it) available for inspection at his offices or, 'on prior receipt of his expenses in that behalf', post a copy to the person wishing to make the inspection. In practice a copy of the GV79E is sent by post on receipt of a nominal fee.

There is, however, no obligation on a Licensing Authority to inform an objector or representor of an applicant's written response,

---

[6] See p 63. The representor may of course assert that he or she *did* send a copy. If this assertion is made at a Public Inquiry it is usually accepted, as the applicant will be unable to prove the negative. The requirement is to 'send' a copy not 'deliver' it.

through the medium of a GV79E or otherwise. In Appeal 1986 No X27 *Wellingborough Borough Council and W Brown (Leather Goods)* the Licensing Authority had reached his decision to grant a licence on the basis of the written objection and the reply to it without a Public Inquiry and without copying the applicant's written representations to the objecting Council – or even, it seems, informing the Council of their existence. The Council argued that the Licensing Authority had failed to observe the rules of natural justice by not giving them the opportunity to reply to and contest the applicant's representations, including a plan which the Council alleged was misleading. The Tribunal held, after considering Regulation 16 of the 1984 Regulations, SI 1984 No 176, that the Licensing Authority was not in breach of the rule of natural justice: there was no obligation to bring the information to the appellants' attention. ' . . . the onus was upon the appellants to inspect the applications and the supplementary information provided by [the applicants] . . . The appellants were plainly lulled into a false sense of security by their expectation that a Public Inquiry would be held; but that was the result of their own misjudgment, and not of any denial of the rights (sic) of natural justice.'[7]

If indeed that case decides that the existence of a written response to the objection need not be revealed to the objectors before a decision is made, it seems that some reconsideration of the terms of Regulation 16 is called for. Be that as it may, it is the practice (in some Traffic Areas at least), in cases where in the Licensing Authority's judgment the statements in the GV79E provide a *prima facie* answer to the complaints of representors, to direct that copies of it (or parts of it) be sent to them without charge.[8]

The conduct of inquiries

Public Inquiries are held at frequent intervals and are conducted by the Licensing Authority or a Deputy Licensing Authority. Regulation 24 of SI 1984 No 176 requires the Licensing Authority to publish in *A & D,* amongst other things, the dates on which and the places at which he proposes to hold inquiries, and the applications which he proposes to consider there. The applicants, objectors and representors will also be individually advised of the date and venue of any inquiry at which their case is to be heard. Since June 1984 – when the 'environmental' provisions of the Act came into effect – most Licensing Authorities

---

[7] The appeal was allowed on another ground, see p 88.
[8] This involves an element of extra cost, but may well be justified if the holding of a Public Inquiry is thereby avoided.

have felt it necessary to hold the inquiries more locally, ie within an accessible distance from the operating centre involved, to enable representors to attend without too much difficulty or expense.

In cases involving environmental issues, some – if not most – Licensing Authorities and Deputies find it helpful to visit the site to see the operating centre and the immediate vicinity, either before, during or after the hearing. The question of whether they should be unaccompanied, or invite the parties and/or their representatives to be present depends on the circumstances of each case. The only rule which applies to all cases is that if the Licensing Authority draws any conclusions from what he observes he must inform all the parties of (a) the facts he has observed and (b) any conclusions he is disposed to draw from those facts, [9] and give them the opportunity to contest the facts and make submissions about the conclusions. For this reason – namely that he must not base his decision on evidence (ie his own observations) not disclosed to all the parties – it is perhaps preferable for the site visit, if any, to be made before or during the hearing and not after it has been concluded.

There are no detailed rules governing the conduct of inquiries. Regulation 23(3) provides that 'a Licensing Authority may regulate the procedure of any inquiry which he holds under section 69(9) or 87, and may, in particular and without prejudice to the foregoing provisions of this paragraph, exclude any submission or evidence on the ground that he considers it to be vexatious, frivolous or irrelevant.' The 'foregoing provisions' relate to the extent to which persons have the right to appear at an inquiry, or may be excluded from it by the Licensing Authority. Regulation 23(2) provides:

> '(2) At an inquiry held by a Licensing Authority in relation tc an application for a licence or a variation of a licence any person who is:
> (a) the applicant,
> (b) a person who has objected to the application,
> (c) a person who has duly made representations in respect of the application, or
> (d) a person referred to in section 69(9) who has requested the inquiry,
> shall be entitled to appear at the inquiry and either be heard in person or represented by Counsel, a solicitor or, at the discretion of the Licensing Authority, by any other representative.'
> representative.'

It may be noted that sub-paragraph (d) appears out of place in a paragraph dealing with inquiries about applications because section

---

[9] For instance he may consider a representor's house to be too far from the operating centre to be affected by noise etc.

69(9) relates only to inquiries into action proposed by the Licensing Authority against an existing licence-holder; this subject is dealt with on pp 93 – 6. Be that as it may, the immediately preceding paragraph 23(1) provides that where the inquiry relates to the appropriate financial standing of an applicant, attendance may be restricted 'in such manner as the Licensing Authority directs' provided that a member of the Council on Tribunals or its Scottish Committee shall be entitled to attend.[10] The intention of this provision seems clear enough, namely to enable evidence of the financial affairs of an applicant to be heard in camera in compliance or in harmony with the provisions of section 87(5) of the 1968 Act. This section makes it an offence for any person to disclose information with respect to any particular trade or business which is given at any inquiry 'while admission to the inquiry is restricted in accordance with regulations', except with the consent of the person carrying on the trade or business, or for certain statutory purposes.

In appeal 1984 No V7 *Wilkinson Freight (UK) Ltd* the Road Haulage Association lodged an objection on the ground that the applicants did not, and would not, have sufficient financial resources; the Association were represented at the inquiry by a solicitor. The Licensing Authority agreed to a request by the applicants that the financial evidence be heard in private, and excluded (among others) the objectors' solicitor, acting under the powers contained in Regulation 10(1) of the 1977 Regulations, the predecessor of the 1984 Regulations cited above. The Transport Tribunal said: 'Although we have not heard argument on this point our clear provisional view is that there was no power to exclude from any part of an inquiry, whether heard in public or private, an objector who had been given the right of appearance by paragraph (2). The reference to members of the Council on Tribunals at the end of paragraph (1) was necessary, as without it he could have been excluded as a member of the public without any right of appearance under paragraph (2). These regulations have from June 1st 1984 been superseded by the Goods Vehicles (Operators' Licences, Qualifications and Fees) Regulations 1984, SI 1984 No 176. Although the wording of Regulation 23(1) and (2) which takes the place of Regulation 10(1) and (2) of the 1977 Regulations is different, we consider that there is no power to exclude an objector from any part of an inquiry.'[11]

---

[10] The Council on Tribunals was established under the Tribunals and Inquiries Act 1971 to oversee the operation of various tribunals including licensing authorities.

[11] Regulation 10(1) of the 1977 regulations reads as follows:

'10(1) An inquiry or any part of an inquiry held by a Licensing Authority in connection with an application, being an inquiry or part of an inquiry into the

Although this expression of opinion was incidental and referred only to objectors (there was no right of 'representation' at the date of the original inquiry and decision), it would appear to be, so far as it goes, an authority for the proposition that no objector or representor, whatever their grounds of objection, can be excluded from any part of an inquiry. It remains to be seen whether this view is confirmed in future cases. Meanwhile, whatever may be the strict interpretation of the Regulation, the result seems to be at variance with the intention expressed in section 87(5), referred to above, and an alternative interpretation seems possible. While it is clearly reasonable and in accordance with natural justice that an objector *on financial grounds* should not be excluded, there is no reason why representors, who can oppose an application on limited environmental grounds only, should have an absolute right to be present throughout and learn all about the applicant's business affairs. The argument relating to the member of the Council on Tribunals can also be put in another way: he had to be mentioned, not because he had no right of appearance, but because he had to be excepted from the otherwise absolute discretion of the Licensing Authority.

Subject, therefore, to what may or may not be an overriding power to be exercised in the circumstances of Regulation 23(1), every objector and representor has the right to appear and be heard or represented at a Public Inquiry. For reasons already given (p 53), the right of a representor to appear may still be challenged on the ground that he or she is not qualified under section 69B(2), or has not fully complied with Regulations 18 and 19. The Licensing Authority should not admit the evidence of a representor who is not properly qualified, even if the applicant makes no objection (see p53), but in practice the evidence is usually taken provisionally, with the ruling on admissibility given as part of the decision. The representor's right under Regulation 23(2) is to appear *and* to be *either* heard *or* represented. The intention presumably is that the representor should give his or her evidence personally, but this is not yet entirely clear. A representative cannot give evidence, but may perhaps be allowed to read out the letter of representation, base submissions on it, and

---

financial resources which are or are likely to be available to the applicant, shall be held in private if the Licensing Authority so directs at the request of the applicant, but a member of the Council on Tribunals or its Scottish Committee shall be entitled to attend the hearing in his capacity as such member'.

With minor verbal differences (eg 'appropriate financial standing' instead of 'financial resources') Regulation 23(2) of 1984 SI 176 is to the same effect, except that the words 'at the request of the applicant' are omitted, thus enlarging the discretion of the Licensing Authority.

cross-examine the applicant (provided the cross-examiner does not assume facts outside those stated in the letter) in the absence of the representor. A Department of Transport booklet (GV74R) entitled *A Guide to Making Representations* implies that the representative may attend and put forward the representor's case on his or her behalf, although he may not 'stray into wider issues'. There must clearly be a limit to the extent to which a representative – especially one claiming to represent a number of residents – can put forward hearsay evidence and base arguments upon it, in the absence of the original representors, whom the applicant will not be able to cross-examine.

Regulation 23(2) applies equally to objectors, both in cases under section 63 and section 69B(1). It is usual for Councils to be represented by an official in the legal or administrative section who calls one or more technical officers as witnesses, but it occasionally happens that one officer will combine the roles of advocate and witness, both giving the evidence and making submissions upon it. In such a case it is important to distinguish clearly the two capacities in which he appears. In Appeal 1983 No U2 *John Edward Gray* v. *West Yorkshire Metropolitan County Council* the Tribunal said: 'It is desirable that where a person appearing as or for an applicant or an objector has the combined role of witness and advocate, his or her two functions should be kept separate. Such a person should be asked to give evidence and then be cross-examined before he or she argues the applicant's case and makes submissions.'

Normally in civil cases the party bearing the onus of proof – that is to say in this context the objectors – have the right and duty to begin. In goods operator licensing cases, there being no formal pleadings, objectors and more especially representors will not know more than a bare outline of the application. It will normally be convenient, therefore, for the applicant's case to be opened at the start of the hearing, without evidence being given, to be followed by the evidence of the objectors and/or the representors. The applicant, assuming he has a case to answer, will then give his evidence, on which he can be cross-examined by the objectors and representors. In Appeal 1985 No W11 *R G Brimley t/a Retailset* the Transport Tribunal said: '. . . we suggest that where representors are present to oppose an application on environmental grounds there is much to be said for each representor giving evidence and being cross-examined before the appellant gives evidence and is cross-examined by them. Such an order would help the representors to distinguish between their evidence and their questions in cross-examination of the applicant, something which lay people often find very difficult.' (This suggestion was repeated in Appeal 1987 No Y12 *Mid Suffolk District Council* v. *A Dowell Junior.*)

There will of course be cases in which the applicant may have to satisfy the Licensing Authority on matters to which there has been no objection, and which cannot be the subject of representations, eg professional competence or maintenance arrangements. The applicant will have to present his own case on these issues separately from the case arising under section 69B(1) or (2), and the representors, if present, will have no right to cross-examine him on these issues. As will be seen (p 69), the applicant may, even in an environmental case, have to satisfy the Licensing Authority that his application will not involve any 'material change' under section 69B(5).

Regulation 23(4) requires the Licensing Authority, in cases where he refuses an application for the grant or variation of a licence, or grants it otherwise than in the terms applied for, to furnish to the applicant, any objector, and any representor who asks for it, a statement 'either written or oral' of the reasons for his decision. In most cases the decision will be given orally at the end of the hearing, to be followed by a letter confirming it; occasionally the Licensing Authority will reserve the decision and put it and the reasons for it into writing. Normally the written decision or the letter confirming the decision given orally, will be copied only to the representors who appeared at the hearing, but the language of the regulation 'any person who has made a representation in accordance with Regulations 18 and 19' is wide enough to cover those who did not appear, but who may perhaps ask, either before or after the hearing, to be informed of the decision. It is significant in this connection that under the Transport Tribunal Rules 1986, referred to on p 54, a 'proper officer' of the Tribunal must send a notice of every appeal to each representor, defined as meaning 'a person who duly made representations under section 69B or 69D of the 1968 Act against the application for, or for the variation of, the operator's licence in question.[12]

There seems to be no statutory requirement for the reasons to be supplied to objectors and/or representors where the application is granted in spite of their objections and/or representations. In practice copies of the decision or decision letter are supplied in the same way as in the previous situation; in any case, since objectors have a right of appeal, they will have to be informed of the reasons for the decision which they may wish to challenge. This point was dealt with in Appeal 1986 No X11 *D H Lodge (t/a Tiptree Union Haulage)*; the Deputy Licensing Authority had announced his decision, without giving reasons, although various issues had been

[12] The implications of this regulation will be further considered in Chapter 9.

left for his determination. He gave his reasons in the form of 'observations' on the Notice of Appeal. The Transport Tribunal said: 'The Notice of Appeal produced what is in effect a written judgment by the Deputy Licensing Authority justifying his decision. We have in earlier judgments said that this is an undesirable practice and that Licensing Authorities and their Deputies should normally make findings of fact and explain their decision at or within a reasonable time of holding a Public Inquiry rather than produce the only reasoned judgment under the guise of "observations" on receipt of the Notice of Appeal.'[13]

---

[13] The reference is to rule 13(1)(c) of the Transport Tribunal Rules 1986 SI No 1546, which requires the Licensing Authority to send to the Tribunal a statement of his reasons for the decision appealed against. See also Appeal 1987 No Y12 *Mid Suffolk District Council* v. *A Dowell Junior (Trading as A Dowell & Sons (Bury))*.

CHAPTER 5

Principles of Environmental Suitability

The essential object of the amendments introduced by the 1982 Act, and applicable to licences granted on applications lodged on or after 1 June 1984, as stated in the heading and side-note to section 52, is the environmental control of goods vehicle operating centres. The powers given to the Licensing Authority relate solely to the operating centre and its 'vicinity'; he has no power to control the movement or routeing of goods vehicles generally. The new definition of 'operating centre' and some of the difficulties arising from it have been discussed already (see p 45). The first two or three appeal judgments by the Transport Tribunal underlined the limitations inherent in the Licensing Authority's jurisdiction. In Appeals 1984 Nos V22 *UK Corrugated Ltd* and V21 *Auto Industries Ltd* (decided in that date order), the following principles were stated:

(1) a vehicle's operating centre is where the vehicle normally stands when it is not being used, and the Licensing Authority has to be satisfied that the place is suitable for that purpose (only);

(2) the only vehicles whose parking, movement or other activity can be taken into account are the vehicles 'authorised' under the licence.[1] Whatever prejudicial effects may be produced at or near the operating centre by other than authorised vehicles are not to be taken into account. This is so even if the 'visiting vehicles', by temporarily occupying the operating centre, compel the authorised vehicles to obstruct the highway outside.[2]

As regards (1), the gloss put on the definition by the words 'when . . . not being used', which do not appear in the Act or Regulations, is no doubt justified by the expression 'normally kept',

[1] ie authorised by virtue of section 61(1) of the 1968 Act.
[2] But see now the discussion of these principles in Appeal 1985 No W17 *Surrey Heath Borough Council* v. *NFT Distribution Ltd*, on p 53.

and the words in parenthesis in section 52(1): ' . . . (whether or not it [the authorised vehicle] is also normally used from there) . . .'. The expression 'normally stands when...not being used' used by the Tribunal cannot however imply that all that needs to be considered is the effect produced by an authorised vehicle standing motionless with its engine switched off – which would presumably be a matter of visual intrusion only – since not only would it be contrary to the clear intention of the Act, but it is also untenable in the light of later appeal decisions, where movement of authorised vehicles both within, and into and out of the operating centre, have been treated as relevant. An example is Appeal 1985 No W13 *Carryfast Ltd*, which was allowed in part by the Tribunal on the grounds that although there was evidence of movement of authorised vehicles into and out of the operating centre, there was no evidence of movement within it. It is the case, however, that movement as such is not essential: in Appeal 1985 No W17 *Surrey Heath Borough Council* v. *NFT Distribution Ltd* the use of an auxiliary engine fitted to and forming part of the use of an authorised vehicle for the purpose of refrigeration was held to be 'clearly part of the use of the operating centre', and the noise it made could be taken into account.

The limitation of the jurisdiction to cover 'authorised' vehicles only is established by **section 52(2)** of the 1982 Act, which states that the provision in Part I of Schedule 4 (ie sections 69A to 69G added to the 1968 Act) 'establish control by Licensing Authorities under Part V of the Transport Act 1968 over

> (a) the places which may be used as operating centres for authorised vehicles under goods vehicle operators' licences granted under that Part of the Act; and
> (b) the use to which any such centre may be put for authorised vehicles under any operator's licence so granted . . .'

Experience has shown that in a significant proportion of cases the complaints of local residents about the operating centre relate not to the licence-holder's authorised vehicles, but to vehicles which visit his premises on business, and which may be both larger and more numerous than the operator's own vehicles (as, for instance, in Appeal 1985 No W11 *R G Brimley*).

Material change

Section 69B(5) of the 1968 Act as amended by the 1982 Act provides as follows:

'(5) A Licensing Authority may not refuse an application for an operator's licence under subsection (4) of this section [ie on environmental grounds] if the applicant satisfies the authority that the grant of the application will not result in any material change as regards

(a) the places in the area of the authority used or to be used as operating centres for authorised vehicles under any operator's licence previously granted by the authority or under the licence applied for;[3] or

(b) the use of any such place already in use as an operating centre under an existing licence so granted.'

The subsection in effect requires the applicant to show *both* that the place or places are the same as those used under a previous licence *and* that the use is or will be essentially the same as under an existing licence. It has been argued that since the provisions are expressed in the alternative it is sufficient to show that paragraph (a) alone is satisfied. This argument was dismissed by the Transport Tribunal in Appeal 1985 No W12 *J Cryer & Sons Ltd* in the following terms: 'That proposition is in our judgment unsustainable when the terms of the whole subsection are properly considered. If correct it would mean that however vast were the proposed changes in the use of the operating centre a Licensing Authority could not refuse a licence under subsection (4) if the location and structure of the operating centre remained without material change.'

Since both paragraphs have to be satisfied, it would follow that for the plea of 'no material change' to succeed, there must in every case be an existing licence covering the use of the operating centre. Given that paragraph (b) must be satisfied in every case, it would not be enough to show that the place was used as an operating centre in the past, and that the use now proposed to be made of it is no greater than was made at that time. This view was confirmed in Appeal 1986 No X29 *Kirk Brothers Ltd* v. *Macclesfield Borough Council and Others*, where the Transport Tribunal stated: 'It is clear that under that section [sc. s.69B(5)] the Licensing Authority is not concerned with use as an operating centre in the past under a licence which has come to an end.' They added later in the judgment that even if that

---

[3] The last six words are obscure, as the comparison being made is between what is applied for and what existed in the past. As to the meaning of 'previously granted', see Appeal 1986 No X29 *Kirk Brothers Ltd* v. *Macclesfield Borough Council*, referred to above.

were not so, 'the weight to be given by the Licensing Authority to Regulation 22(1)(b)[4] in reaching his decision would be minimal having regard to the intervening years. The mere fact that Smithy Garage had an established use certificate for use for haulage and storage under planning law is in our judgment immaterial.'[5]

The question of what constitutes a material change in the use of the operating centre is a matter for the judgment of the Licensing Authority, provided that his decision is not one at which no reasonable licensing authority could have arrived. (See Appeal 1985 No W12 *J Cryer & Sons Ltd*). It was held in Appeal 1985 No W30 *Strathkelvin District Council* v. *Fife Forwarding Company Ltd* that in considering whether there has been or will be a material change the Licensing Authority can take into account only the use of the place by authorised vehicles under the licence, leaving out of account its use by other vehicles or in other ways. However, the Tribunal, in Appeal 1986 No X17 *David Hugh Wylie (t/a Sunnyside Removals)*, held that they had been wrong so to decide in *Strathkelvin*, and came to the conclusion that 'section 69B(5)(b) requires a Licensing Authority to have regard to all uses to which a place already in use as an operating centre is put in deciding whether the grant of the application will result in a material change of use'. In effect, therefore, he must approach the question of 'use' in a more general way, and decide whether the grant of the application would have such an effect on the overall use of the operating centre as to amount to a 'material change of use' in planning terms. It will obviously be important for the Licensing Authority to know – or if necessary decide – precisely what is comprised in the 'operating centre' considered as a planning unit, and what the existing use or uses are. Indeed, the Tribunal recommended in the *Sunnyside* case that if there is any doubt on the matter, the applicant should be required to supply an up-to-date scale plan clearly defining the boundaries of the operating centre.

One possible consequence of the ruling in *Sunnyside* is that 'material change of use' will be less easy to establish, since the change in goods vehicle licensing terms may not amount to a material change of use in planning (or 'overall use') terms. Other things being equal, own account operators, whose transport operations are by definition only a part of their total business, may be better placed than hauliers to satisfy the Licensing Authority on 'no material change'.

---

[4] Sc. of the 1984 Regulations SI 176. Regulation 22(1)(b) relates to considerations of material change in the determination of environmental issues. See pp 78 – 9.

[5] The immateriality of established use certificates to operator licensing was restated in Appeal 1987 No Y12 *Mid Suffolk District Council* v. *A Dowell Junior*.

As to the nature of material change in itself, it seems plain that it is not limited to an increase in the number of authorised vehicles normally kept at the operating centre; it might consist in the introduction of night operations, an increase in the number of arrivals and departures, or the opening of a new point of ingress and egress, to give some examples. It is suggested that where it was shown that the only change was an increase in the size of the authorised vehicles, or the substitution, say, of articulated combinations for smaller rigid vehicles, this could constitute a material change, as would the addition of trailers to the licence, even if such changes could have been made lawfully, and without the opportunity for objection, under the previous licence. Similarly, it is an open question whether the intention to fill up a margin of two or three vehicles which was available but not used on the previous licence would constitute making a material change in the use of the operating centre. If the issue has to be determined, the burden is on the applicant to satisfy the Licensing Authority that there will be no material change.

The statutory rule that an application involving no material change may not be refused on environmental grounds may have a direct bearing on the decision of the Licensing Authority on an original application, against which objections or representations have been lodged. The Licensing Authority has to bear in mind that if he is disposed to grant the application – perhaps for a short term to see whether the anticipated prejudical effects do in fact occur – he will be precluded from refusing a renewal application if there is then no material change, even if the operations have in fact been environmentally undesirable. In Appeal 1986 No X27 *Wellingborough Borough Council and W Brown (Leather Goods)*, the facts of which are set out on p 60, the Transport Tribunal said: ' . . . Thus if Mr Brown were to apply for a renewal of the licence upon its expiry 2 years hence, and if, as seems highly likely, he was then able to satisy the Licensing Authority that the renewal of the licence would not result in any material change in the use of the operating centre as such, the Licensing Authority would not be able to refuse the grant of the licence on environmental grounds, unless he was satisfied that the parking of the authorised vehicle at or in the vicinity of the operating centre would cause adverse effects on environmental conditions in the vicinity – see section 69B(3). It is certainly not clear from his decision whether the Licensing Authority had the effect of section 69B(5) in mind when limiting the licence to a two-year period. On the contrary, the final paragraph of his decision suggests that he thought that he would be able to reconsider the grant of the licence in the light of the appellant's objections when it came up for renewal. If that interpretation of his decision is correct he plainly fell into error and granted the licence upon an erroneous basis.' The application was accordingly remitted to the Licensing Authority for consideration in the light of this judgment.[6]

It was for long uncertain whether a so-called 'interim' grant would have the same effect, seeing that a grant made under section 67(5) is of a 'licence', albeit one expressed to continue for a limited if uncertain period.[7] The question has, however, been settled by Appeal 1986 No X29 *Kirk Brothers Ltd* v. *Macclesfield Borough Council and Others,* in which the Tribunal stigmatised as 'absurd' an interpretation of section 69B(5) which prevented a Licensing Authority who had granted an 'interim' licence from refusing the substantive application on grounds of 'no material change', when he had never had to consider the requirements of section 64, and there had been no opportunity for objections or representations.

Conditions under section 69C

Where refusal of the application on environmental grounds is precluded by section 69B(5) the Licensing Authority may impose conditions under section 69C[8], but before doing so he is required by section 69C(5) to give the applicant an opportunity to make representations concerning the effect on his business of any conditions the Authority proposes to attach, and to give a special consideration to those representations. The procedures to be adopted to give effect to these rules have been considered in several appeals,[9] and may be summarised as follows. The Licensing Authority should put the proposed conditions in writing, and give the applicant time to consider them and prepare his representations, consulting with his accountant or solicitor as necessary. This will normally involve an adjournment, and consideration of written representations, and/or a further hearing.[10] Giving 'special consideration' apparently means

---

[6]   See also 1987 No Y12 *Mid Suffolk District Council* v. *A Dowell Junior.*
[7]   For an explanation of 'interim' licences, see p 14.
[8]   The kind of conditions which may be imposed, and their enforcement, will be dealt with in detail in Chapter 6, pp 000ff. It will be appropriate to complete the consideration of 'material change' by dealing with s.69C(5) in this chapter.
[9]   Appeal 1985 No W7 *Thrapston Warehousing Ltd*;
      Appeal 1985 No W8 *Roger Graham Bown t/a R G B Transport*;
      Appeal 1985 No W14 *Ron Chalker (The Potato Man) Ltd*;
      Appeal 1985 No W19 *M and G House*;
      Appeal 1986 No X1 *C Smith t/a A.1 Demolition.*
[10] See Appeal 1986 No X1 *C Smith t/a A.1 Demolition*:
      'There is no statutory requirement that representations made under section 69C(5) should be supported by oral evidence.'

examining the representations with particular care, and stating all the facts found which are relevant to the decision (if made) to impose conditions. In Appeal 1985 No W14 *Ron Chalker (The Potato Man) Ltd* the Tribunal observed that there might be conditions which it would be reasonable to impose when the grant of the application would result in a material change in the use of the operating centre but which it would not be reasonable to impose where there was no such material change. 'In such circumstances the effect of the proposed conditions on an existing business required particularly close scrutiny and must receive special consideration.'

One of the most instructive judgments on this topic was Appeal 1985 No W8 *Roger Graham Bown t/a R G B Transport* in which the application was one for the variation of a licence. In that case the Tribunal ruled that section 69B(5) applied to variations equally with applications for a licence. In a subsequent case[11] they decided that the 'no material change' rule did *not* apply to variation applications, as section 69D contains no provision analogous to section 69B(5). The conflict was resolved in Appeal 1986 No X10 *Ken Abram Ltd* v. *West Lancashire District Council*, when the Tribunal decided to follow *D & A Transport*, ie held that section 69B(5) did *not* apply to variation applications. As the Transport Tribunal are not bound by their own decisions,[12] the question is perhaps still open for argument. Clearly a variation to add vehicles is inherently likely to involve a material change; but where operator A wishes to vary his licence by exchanging his operating centre for one vacated by operator B, he should perhaps be able to take advantage of the 'established use' if in fact there is no material change.[13]

It is uncertain whether the further representations, if made in writing, have to be copied to objectors and/or representors, and whether the latter have any right to make counter-representations. It would appear *prima facie* that, the Licensing Authority having acceded to the objections or representations to the extent of proposing conditions (when, following the stated hypothesis there is no material change in the use of the operating centre), the final stage, with or without a further hearing, takes place between the applicant and the Licensing Authority. Certainly it has been assumed in practice that any further hearing to give special consideration to the representations would involve only the one side, excluding any

[11] Appeal 1985 No W23 *D & A Transport Ltd and Others* v. *Lancashire County Council and Another*.
[12] See, for example, Appeal 1981 No S11 *William North Curtis*, citing *Merchandise Transport Ltd* v. *British Transport Commission* (1962) 2 QB 173.
[13] See Appeal 1985 W16 *BRS (Southern) Ltd* v. *Canterbury City Council* where the facts were similar. It was assumed in that case that the 'no material change' rule applied.

objectors or representors. In Appeal 1985 No X8 *R Rudge & Sons Limited* the course of the proceedings before the Licensing Authority was described as follows: 'The proposed conditions were set out in the letter, and the Licensing Authority invited the appellants to make representations to him as to the effect of such conditions upon their business. Such representations were made at a further hearing, held in Chambers ...' The Licensing Authority in fact heard further evidence in Chambers from the operator and his accountants. The implication clearly is that the original representors, three of whom had given evidence at the Public Inquiry, were not heard, or even invited to attend, at the hearing in Chambers. No suggestion was made by the Tribunal that this procedure was in any way defective. However, in Appeal 1986 No X10 *West Lancashire District Council* v. *Ken Abram Ltd* it was strenuously argued by the appellant Council that the 'special consideration' hearing in Chambers by the Licensing Authority was not conducted in accordance with the principles of natural justice in that neither the objectors nor the representors were given an opportunity to attend. The Transport Tribunal did not determine this issue, because having decided that on the facts of the case (which was an application to vary a licence) the rules as to 'no material change' did not apply, they found it unnecessary to do so. Meanwhile it may be remarked that the provision was inserted in the Act to protect operators from having stringent conditions imposed in situations where refusal is precluded because of no material change. It can be fairly argued, therefore, that any doubt about the procedure should be resolved in their favour. There are equally strong arguments, based on principle, that issues which concern all the parties to the case should not be heard and resolved without their having an opportunity to attend.

The question arose in a slightly ambiguous context in Appeal 1986 No X34 *R G and M T Jury (t/a R & G Transport)* v. *Devon County Council*. The Deputy Licensing Authority in granting the application clearly stated that there was a material change involved. Nevertheless he (wrongly) concluded that he was required to give the applicants an opportunity to make representations about the effect on their business of certain proposed conditions, and held a Public Inquiry for this purpose. The representors who had appeared at the first inquiry were told that they would not be invited to attend the second, and that they had no right to 'have a say' on the financial and other matters which the Authority would be considering. The Tribunal said: 'We know of no provision in the legislation which prevented him, as he believed and said, from hearing any submissions or representations from the objectors or representors at the Public Inquiry. Neither is there any statutory provision entitling an objector or representor to take part in a Public Inquiry.[14] A Licensing Authority is given a very wide discretion by section 87(1) which states "A Licensing Authority may hold such inquiries as he thinks necessary for the proper exercise of his functions under this part of this Act".' They went on to say: 'If the Deputy Licensing Authority had not misinterpreted the legislation [ie by concluding that he could not hear the representors again at the resumed Public Inquiry] we would have expected him at the least to have permitted cross-examination of Mr Jury by or on behalf of the representors and/or objectors and to have heard submissions by them or on their behalf as to the weight to be attached to Mr Jury's evidence.' In the result the Tribunal dismissed the operator's appeal against the conditions imposed, and awarded costs to representors who had been made parties.[15]

The question needs to be resolved whether there is any difference, so far as the rights of objectors and/or representors are concerned, between a case in which section 69C(5) applies – ie consideration of representations by the applicant is obligatory – and one in which it does not, but the Licensing Authority in his discretion wishes to have the inquiry resumed for further evidence or argument.

A note on parking

An existing operator applying to renew his licence without any material change is not protected by section 69B(5) if the objectors and/or representors can show that 'the parking of authorised vehicles under the licence at or in the vicinity of any place which, if the licence were granted, would be an operating centre of the holder of the licence would cause adverse effects on environmental conditions in the vicinity of that place' :- section 69B(3). The power to refuse an application under section 69B(4) does not extend to refusal on the grounds of parking by section 69B(3), as this ground is specifically excluded, although as the Transport Tribunal pointed out in Appeal 1985 No W23 *D & A Transport and Others* v. *Lancashire County Council and Ribble Borough Council,* refusal of an application under section 69B(3) is also a refusal on an environmental ground. The choice of 'parking' as a matter of such potential damage to the environment as to constitute a separate ground for refusal outside the discretionary powers in section 69B(4)

---

[14] It is not clear why, given that the second Public Inquiry was in the circumstances a continuation of the first, the provisions of Regulation 23(2) did not apply to give the representors that entitlement: see p 61.

[15] For the question of costs, see p 134.

as well as outside the protection of section 69B(5) was, as has been seen, the subject of comment by the Transport Tribunal in Appeal 1985 No W17 *Surrey Heath Borough Council* v. *NFT Distribution Ltd*. Since the Tribunal later, in the *D & A Transport* appeal, rejected as erroneous the interpretation of 'parking' as including the *act* of parking vehicles – which would involve manoeuvring, 'revving' of engines etc – the only environmental effect of parking as a static condition would appear to be visual intrusion or perhaps obstruction of the highway.

One of the matters which the Licensing Authority may regulate by conditions under Regulation 21 is the parking arrangements to be provided for authorised vehicles at or in the vicinity of an operating centre; indeed section 69C(2) specifically includes 'parking arrangements' as one of the matters to be covered by conditions. Since by hypothesis section 69B(5) does not apply to potential refusals on the grounds of parking, a condition imposed to regulate parking arrangements would presumably not be governed by section 69C(5) so as to require representations and special consideration, but this cannot be said to be free from doubt.

Considerations for the determination of environmental questions

Section 69G(3) provides that in making any determination

(a) as to the suitability of an operating centre on environmental grounds;
(b) as to the imposition or variation of any conditions under section 69C;
(c) as to the effect on local environmental conditions of the use of an operating centre

the Licensing Authority shall have regard to certain prescribed considerations. These are set out in Regulation 22 of the 1984 Regulations, SI 1984 No 176, and will be examined in order below. As already noted (p 47), these considerations do not assist the Licensing Authority in coming to a decision on what are the central issues in every 'environmental' case, namely what is the nature and extent of the prejudical effects, if any, of the use of the operating centre, and what is the proper order to make having regard to the interests of all parties. Some general guidance may be said to be given in the Act, namely the provision protecting established use when there is no material change, and the emphasis placed on the effect of conditions on the applicant's business. The Licensing Authority will not lightly take action which will prevent an existing operator from carrying on his business and earning a living, or impose conditions which unduly restrict his operations. Licensing Authorities recognise that people living in areas where there are industrial or commercial activities – which are likely to use goods transport – must expect some interference with their peace and quiet. In many cases compromises can be reached by means of conditions, eg relating to hours of operation, parking arrangements and so on.

Decisions reached *bona fide* after a careful hearing of all sides of a case will not normally be altered on appeal; indeed, the Transport Tribunal in Appeal 1985 No W12 *J Cryer & Sons Ltd* emphasised that 'it is not the practice of the Tribunal to allow appeals as to conditions imposed by a Licensing Authority unless it is shown that the Licensing Authority has misdirected himself as to the law or evidence or has taken into account something which he should not have taken into account or left out of account something he should have taken into account'. In other words the Tribunal are not re-hearing the case on the merits. They do, however, insist on a clear statement by the Licensing Authority of the facts found and the conclusions drawn from them.[16]

Regulation 22(1)

This sets out in paragraphs (a) to (h) the considerations prescribed as relevant to the determination which the Licensing Authority has to make.

'(a) the nature and use of any other land in the vicinity of the land used or proposed to be used as an operating centre, and any effect which the use of the land as an operating centre has or, in the case of application for a licence, would be likely to have, on the environment of that vicinity.'

The Licensing Authority will presumably form a view as to the nature and use of the land in general terms, eg that it is agricultural, or residential, or industrial, or a mixture of two or more as the case may be. He will not be bound by the planning authority's categorisation of it.[17] His conclusion may be of some relevance if the proposed operating centre is new, or a variation to intensify the operation is proposed. The expression 'land in the vicinity' is to be interpreted

[16] Appeal 1985 No W12 *J Cryer & Sons Ltd*;
Appeal 1985 No W14 *Ron Chalker (The Potato Man) Ltd*.
[17] Appeal 1985 No W4 *R A Nightingale t/a Anglia Fruiterers*.

more widely than the same expression in section 69B(2) which, as already pointed out (p 49), is there used to define the right to appear (*locus*) of would-be representors. Furthermore, the reference to 'the environment of the vicinity' arguably indicates a further extension of the area which may be prejudicially affected. In the *Hay & Straw Servi*ces case,[18] The Transport Tribunal decided that, on an objection by a statutory objector under section 69B(1), the Licensing Authority must, for example, take into account the effects produced by the authorised vehicles moving on approach roads. The distance from the operating centre to which environmental considerations may extend is nevertheless still limited, it is suggested, by the concept that any prejudicial effect must arise from the use of the land *as an operating centre,* which by definition and on the basis of the appeal decisions, means use as a place for normally keeping vehicles when not in use (see p 50).

> '(b) in a case where the land proposed to be used as an operating centre is, or has previously been, used as an operating centre, the extent to which the grant of the application would result in any material change as regards that operating centre, or its use, which would adversely affect the environment of the vicinity of that land;
>
> (c) in the case of an application which, if granted, would result in land which has not previously been used as an operating centre being used as one, any information known to the Licensing Authority to whom the application is made about any planning permission or application for planning permission relating to the land or any other land in the vicinity of that land.'

These two paragraphs are set out together because they are mutually exclusive, and only one will apply in a given case. If paragraph (b) applies, and there is or will be a material change, clearly the extent or degree of that change will be relevant. The length of time which has elapsed since the land was 'previously used' will also be relevant, at any rate if there has been no licence in existence authorising its use as an operating centre in the meantime. In Appeal 1986 No X29 *Kirk Brothers Ltd* v. *Macclesfield Borough Council and Others* the Tribunal observed that 'the weight to be given by the Licensing Authority to Regulation 22(1)(b) in reaching his decision would be minimal having regard to the intervening years' – about ten in that case.

A literal interpretation would suggest that it is the effect on the environment of the material change which is relevant, and not the

---

[18] Appeal 1986 No X25.

effect of the whole operation resulting from the change; but the Tribunal has made it clear that the Licensing Authority must consider the whole of the new situation arising as a result of the change. In the *NFT* case[19] the Tribunal held that the Licensing Authority had erred in (as they found) taking into account the adverse environmental effect of only the additional vehicles applied for instead of the total of all the vehicles which would be authorised if the variation was granted. In any event, it is the material change 'as regards the operating centre or its use' which has to be considered, and not changes outside the operating centre, eg the fact that a housing estate has been built close to it.

Where (c) applies, ie the land has not been previously used as an operating centre, the Licensing Authority will be concerned with planning permissions or applications for planning permission, if any, as well as with the general land use position under paragraph (a). Where an actual grant or refusal of planning permission is relevant to the proposed use as an operating centre, the Licensing Authority is likely to be guided by it in reaching his decision, on the ground that the environmental effect has already been considered and weighed in the light of local reactions. If an application for a relevant planning permission is pending, the Licensing Authority may well decide to await the result before determining the licence application.

A mere absence of planning permission, frequently relied upon by local authorities and representors as a ground for objection, is not by itself a relevant factor. In Appeal 1985 No W 21 *Basildon Council and Rees Haulage,* the Transport Tribunal said: ' ... the appellants [the Council] criticised the decision upon the basis that the Licensing Authority failed to have proper regard to sub-paragraph (c) of Regulation 22(1). He heard evidence that there was no relevant planning permission relating to the use of the land; nor had any application for planning permission for change of use been made to the planning authority. However, the land is situated within the Green Belt, and the Licensing Authority was informed that the Council took the view that its use as an operating centre would amount to a breach of planning control. He was told that if he granted the application and Rees Haulage began to use the land as an operating centre, the Council would have to consider the issue of an Enforcement Notice. The Licensing Authority, correctly in our view, decided to disregard the question of enforcement proceedings. To have done otherwise would have been to usurp the functions of the planning authority'. They added that 'the Licensing Authority does

---

[19] Appeal 1985 W17 *Surrey Heath Borough Council* v. *NFT Distribution Ltd.*

not exercise his statutory function to assist the planning authority'.[20]
In Appeal 1987 No Y12 *Mid Suffolk District Council* v. *A Dowell
Junior* the Tribunal emphasised that planning considerations other
than those prescribed by regulation 22(1)(c) in the circumstances
there set out, are irrelevant to the environmental issues; in particular
the existence or absence of an Established Use Certificate will
normally be wholly immaterial.[21]

'(d) the number, type and size of authorised vehicles;
(e) the arrangements for the parking of authorised vehicles or,
in the case of an application for a licence, the proposed or likely
arrangements for such parking.'

These are clearly matters which the Licensing Authority would have
to consider in any case. The question of parking at or in the vicinity
of the operating centre has been discussed in the context of sections
69B(3) and (5) (pp 69 – 72); parking beyond the 'vicinity' of the
operating centre would be irrelevant as not relating to the 'use of the
operating centre as such'.

'(f) the nature and the times of the use of the land for the
purpose of an operating centre or, in the case of an application
for a licence, the proposed nature and times of the use of the
land proposed to be used for that purpose;
(g) the nature and the times of the use of any equipment
installed on the land used as an operating centre for the purpose
of the use of that land as an operating centre or, in the case of
an application for a licence, of any equipment proposed or
likely to be installed on the land proposed to be used as an
operating centre for that purpose.'

The nature of the use of the land for the purpose of an operating
centre must by definition be use as a place to 'normally keep' the
authorised vehicles 'when not in use'. What is intended is presumably
the nature of the activities incidental to that use, eg the running of
engines or manoeuvring of vehicles in the process of arriving,
departing or moving within the site, eg for the purpose of loading
and unloading. Whether environmental effects produced by the
operations of loading or unloading, eg noise, bright lights at night
etc, are relevant to the Licensing Authority's decision was left open

[20] This dictum was repeated in Appeal 1986 No X1 *C Smith t/a A1 Demolition*. It is equally
the case that the fact that a local authority has granted planning permission for related
operations on the land will not preclude it from objecting to an application for an
operator's licence there: see Appeal 1986 No X34 *R G & M T Jury (t/a R & G Transport)* v.
Devon County Council.
[21] See also Appeal 1987 No Y26 *Kirklees Metropolitan Council* v. *Geoffrey Beaumont*, where
the Tribunal upheld the Licensing Authority's rejection of the Council's objections based
on absence of planning permission and conflict with the Green Belt policy.

in Appeal 1985 No W17 *Surrey Heath Borough Council* v. *NFT Distribution Ltd.*

As regards equipment installed on the land, it must be so installed for the purpose of the use of the land as an operating centre, ie as a place to 'normally keep' the vehicles; while there is as yet no authority on the point, presumably such things as fuel tanks and pumps, equipment for washing vehicles, and compressors, for example, for removing wheel nuts or similar purposes, would qualify as relevant.

> '(h) the means and frequency of vehicular ingress to and egress from the land used as an operating centre or, in the case of an application for a licence, the proposed means and frequency of such ingress to and egress from, the land proposed to be used as an operating centre.'

In *Surrey Heath* v. *NFT* the Transport Tribunal said: ' . . we agree that the words "ingress to and egress from the land used as an operating centre" cover only so much of an authorised vehicle's movement on the highway outside the centre as is directly connected with the manoeuvres of entering and leaving the centre.' The 'means' of ingress and egress relate to the physical conformation of the point or points of entry or exit; the 'frequency' relates to the number of arrivals and departures of authorised vehicles, and may be said to be part of the use of the operating centre as such, covered also by paragraph (f) above. The means of ingress to and egress from the operating centre is one of the matters for which conditions can be imposed under Regulation 21 (see p 87 ff).

CHAPTER 6

Variations and Conditions

Variation Applications

Many, perhaps most, of the principles applying to applications for licences apply also to applications to vary existing licences; indeed **section 68(4)** of the 1968 Act provides that so far as applicable and subject to any necessary modifications the provisions of section 64 shall apply to variation applications. The most usual kind of variation application is one to increase the number of authorised vehicles. Other types of variation would be the addition, removal or alteration of conditions under section 66 or, in the context particularly of environmental cases, change of operating centre. An operator may also wish to change a restricted licence into a standard one. The form GV81 on which applications are made provides for any of these kinds of variations to be sought.

Notice of a variation application has to be published in *A & D* in the same way as applications for licences, except in the following cases:

(a) a variation to alter or add to the matters required to be specified for the purpose of a standard licence: in effect, details relating to transport managers;

(b) a variation to convert a restricted to a standard licence;

(c) where the Licensing Authority is satisfied that the application is of so trivial a nature that it is not necessary that an opportunity should be given for objecting to it.

In effect the exceptions in (a) and (b) above mean that changes of transport manager, and conversions of licences from restricted to standard are not open to objections and will be determined by the Licensing Authority at his discretion on the basis of material available to him. The dispensation from publication accorded to these two cases were given by the Goods Vehicles (Operators' Licences, Qualifications and Fees) (Amendment) Regulations 1986 SI 1986 No 666, amending the 1984 Regulations and indirectly amending section 68 itself. Paragraph (c) leaves it to the Licensing

Authority's discretion to decide whether a variation is so trivial as not to require publication. Before 1 June 1984 the only advertisement required was in his own publication, *Applications and Decisions*; since the material to appear in *A & D* is routinely prepared by office staff the Licensing Authority would not normally see an application at an early enough stage to decide whether it should be published or not. It is probable that either the applicant would represent that his application was trivial; or it would fall within the limits of guidance laid down by the Licensing Authority, eg that an addition of less than $x\%$ of fleet numbers was to be treated as trivial. The writer knows of no appeal decisions on the point.

Since 1 June 1984 applicants for variations, like applicants for licences, usually advertise their application in the local newspaper at the same time as or before they lodge the application. It therefore comes to public notice before the Licensing Authority has had an opportunity to consider whether it is 'trivial' within paragraph (c): indeed, representations may already have been made against it. An operator seeking a 'trivial' variation should therefore, it is suggested, send with his application a request that it be treated as 'trivial', and abstain from local advertisement pending the Licensing Authority's decision.

In Appeal 1985 No W8 *Roger Graham Bown (t/a RGB Transport)* the Transport Tribunal linked the question of trivial variation with that of material change, and said: 'In passing we point out that a Licensing Authority does not have to publish every application to vary a licence. Sections 68(4)(c) and 69D(3) provide that he need not do so if he is satisfied that the application is of so trivial a nature that it is not necessary that an opportunity should be given for objecting to it or making representations against it. One of the matters to which a Licensing Authority will, no doubt, direct his mind when considering the application of this exception is whether the variation applied for will result in an material change in the use of the operating centre.'

Section 69D sets out the procedure so far as matters peculiar to operating centres are concerned:

> '69D (1) Subject to section 69E of this Act,[1] on the application of the holder of an operator's licence, the Licensing Authority by whom the licence was granted may at any time while it is in force vary the licence by directing
>
> (a) that a new place shall be specified in the licence as an operating centre of the holder of the licence, or that any place so specified shall cease to be so specified; or

---

[1] This is the section requiring applications to be advertised in a local newspaper.

(b) that any condition attached to the licence under section 69C of this Act shall be varied or removed.

(2) [Duty to provide information.]

(3) The Licensing Authority shall publish in the prescribed manner notice of any application for a variation under this section, unless the Licensing Authority is satisfied that the application is of so trivial a nature that it is not necessary that an opportunity should be given for objecting to it or making representations against it.'

The problem here is the same as before, except that variations under section 69D are of a different kind from those under section 68. It is unlikely that any relevant variation other than one (perhaps) for giving up an existing operating centre, would be regarded as 'trivial'.

It would seem that no appeal can be made to the Transport Tribunal from the decision of a Licensing Authority to treat a variation application as trivial, or the decision to grant it without publication, since (apart from applicants and licence-holders) no person may appeal against the grant of an application who has not 'duly made an objection' to it (Transport Act 1968 s.70(1)(c). It could perhaps be argued that in a case where the applicant had advertised in a local paper before the Licensing Authority had decided to treat the application as trivial, and a local authority had made 'representations', the latter might have to be treated as a duly made objection, following the Transport Tribunal's observations in Appeal 1985 No W30 *Strathkelvin District Council* v. *Fife Forwarding Company Limited* (see p 47).

Conditions

Section 66 of the 1968 Act empowers a Licensing Authority on granting a licence to attach such conditions as he thinks fit, requiring the holder to inform him

(a) of any change, of a kind specified in the condition, in the organisation, management or ownership of the trade or business in the course of which the authorised vehicles are used;

(b) where the holder of the licence is a company, of any change, or of any change so specified, in the persons holding shares in the company;

(c) of any other event so specified affecting the holding of the licence which is relevant to the exercise of any power of the authority in relation to the licence.'

There is a penalty of a fine not exceeding £1000[2] on conviction for contravention of any condition so attached.

This section has been comparatively little used so far as requiring notification of changes in management, ownership or the shareholding of companies is concerned, although a change in control of a company, by take-over or otherwise, may in practice create a wholly new operator, so far as the personalities, records and repute of its directors and shareholders are concerned, none of which may be known to the Licensing Authority. Where such a condition has been imposed, it will presumably be the duty of the successor directors and/or shareholders to report the facts to the Licensing Authority. There is no specific provision in the Act requiring relevant convictions to be reported, although such reporting can be required by a condition under section 66(1)(c); indeed, on the printed form of conditions attached to a restricted licence (OL 2R) there is a condition requiring the holder to notify the Licensing Authority within 28 days of any relevant conviction under section 69(4) of the 1968 Act.

Since 1978, by virtue of the Goods Vehicle Operators (Qualifications) Regulations 1977 SI 1977 No 1462 and the replacement 1984 Regulations SI 1984 No 176, the Licensing Authority has been obliged when granting a standard licence to attach to it:

(a) a condition requiring the holder to inform the Licensing Authority within 28 days of any event affecting his good repute, financial standing or professional competence, and

(b) a condition in the same terms relating to the good repute or professional competence of any transport manager employed as such.

These provisions supplement and do not substitute for those of section 66. Since the imposition is obligatory, conditions are printed on every standard licence (OL 2S) which are evidently intended to fulfil the requirements of the regulations as set out above. In particular the following conditions appear:

'*Transport Manager:* the holder shall notify the Licensing Authority within 28 days if any of the following persons ceases to be employed by the holder as a transport manager. [Here will be inserted the name or names of the transport manager(s) accepted as such, if any.]

Repute: the holder shall inform the Licensing Authority within 28 days of any event which could affect his repute or that of any transport manager in his employment.

---

[2] Section 66(2), as increased to level 4: see note 1, chapter 1.

Financial Standing: the holder shall inform the Licensing Authority within 28 days of any event which could affect his claim to be of appropriate financial standing.'

It will be seen that there is no condition requiring the reporting of any other event affecting professional competence, eg the retirement of the professionally competent partner from a firm. Moreover, it is left to the judgment of the licence-holder whether any particular event affects his repute or his financial standing, and if he could show a genuine belief that a given event, eg a conviction of an employee, or a judgment against him for money owed, could not affect his repute or financial standing, it would appear that he would have a defence against a charge of breach of condition for not reporting it. The Licensing Authority may no doubt add more specific conditions at his discretion, relying on section 66.

Environmental conditions

Section 69D empowers the Licensing Authority to attach conditions to an operator's licence for the purpose of preventing or minimising any adverse effects on environmental conditions arising from the use of an operating centre as such (ie as a place where the authorised vehicles are normally kept). There is no requirement in the Act for an objection or representation to be duly made before conditions may be attached under section 69D, so that the Licensing Authority could act of his own motion if he considered it appropriate to do so. However, he can attach conditions only on granting the licence or on an application by the licence-holder for a variation of the licence, in which case he may add, vary or remove any condition: section 69D(8). There is no power for the Licensing Authority to impose a condition during the currency of the licence, eg at the instance of a statutory objector; nor is there any right for the owners or occupiers of land in the vicinity of an operating centre to request a review of conditions imposed upon an operator's licence.[3] Even where conditions may properly be imposed – ie on applications for a licence or a variation – the Licensing Authority must decide on appropriate conditions on the information put before him, and cannot require the applicant to negotiate the terms of a condition with another authority (eg a planning authority) whose responsibilities are of an entirely different nature.[4]

---

[3] Appeal 1985 No W14 *Ron Chalker (The Potato Man) Ltd.*
[4] Appeal 1986 No X1 *C Smith t/a A1 Demolition.*

It not infrequently happens that an operator opposing the imposition of conditions on the operation of his vehicles will state his intention, if conditions are imposed, of employing as required vehicles on contract to do the work instead of using his own. The activities of such vehicles could not be controlled by conditions on his licence. Licensing Authorities have adopted different responses to this argument. For their part, the Tribunal in Appeal 1987 No Y3 *Eskett Quarries* v. *Dr B Courtney and Others*, treated the question as irrelevant in principle. They said: 'Even if an operator expresses an intention to contract his work out so as to avoid the effect of a condition attached to the licence, that is no reason for not attaching a condition which will help to reduce the adverse environmental effect of the use of vehicles authorised on the licence.'

Although the Licensing Authority by section 69D(1) may attach such conditions 'as appear to him appropriate', he is in fact limited to the four kinds of condition prescribed by Regulation 21, each of which will now be examined.

The prescribed conditions (a), (b), (c) and (d) regulate the following:

> (a) the number, size and type of authorised vehicles which may at any one time be at an operating centre of the holder of the licence in the area of the authority for the purposes of maintenance and parking.

Section 64(4) of the 1968 Act provides generally that the Licensing Authority may grant a licence for fewer vehicles or trailers than applied for, or for vehicles of a different type from those applied for. In the context of environmental considerations he will normally be influenced by the capacity or suitability of the operating centre for the number and kind of vehicles sought to be licenced, and may limit the grant on those grounds. Condition (a) envisages that he may wish to limit the number to be maintained and/or parked there at any one time to a number below the number of vehicles authorised on the licence, which will specify the place in question as the operating centre under section 69A(1). If the licence specifies two or more operating centres, and purports to divide the authorised vehicles between them, a condition under Regulation 21(a) will be necessary to ensure that the numbers allotted to each are not exceeded. In Appeal 1986 No X9 *J F & A J Trezise t/a John Trezise & Sons* a licence had been granted for 5 vehicles at operating centre A and 8 vehicles at operating centre B. The operator was found to be keeping 6 or 7 vehicles at centre A. The Transport Tribunal agreed that in the absence of a condition under Regulation 21(a) it was open to the appellants to keep any of the vehicles on the licence at centre A (or B for that matter).

Other problems arise where the operator, although needing to have a certain number of authorised vehicles for his business, cannot get all of them into his operating centre at once, but explains that a number of them are always away at any one time, and those 'at home' can be accommodated. If a condition is imposed limiting the number under Regulation 21(a), it may well appear that some of the vehicles may have no operating centre. Section 52 of the 1982 Act defined 'operating centre' as meaning 'in relation to any vehicle [in the singular], the base or centre at which it is normally kept'. In the given situation it would seem that of any given vehicle it could be said that when it is not in use it is normally kept at place *X*, although it is only there for half of its time. The Transport Tribunal considered this problem in Appeal 1986 No X11 *D H Lodge (t/a Tiptree Union Haulage)* v. *Colchester Borough Council*. In remitting the case to the Deputy Licensing Authority to consider the appropriateness of a condition under Regulation 21 (a) they observed: 'Before a Licensing Authority imposes a condition limiting the number of vehicles which can at any one time be parked at an operating centre to a smaller number than the total number authorised under the licence, he ought to be satisfied either that the business can be organised in such a way that the extra vehicles authorised under the licence would be in use on the road or that a suitable operating centre for the extra vehicles exists. We have no doubt that one of the aims of this legislation is to prevent the regular parking of vehicles in side streets and outside drivers' houses.'[5]

It may be briefly added that Regulation 21(a) does not empower the Licensing Authority to attach a condition regulating the number of vehicles that may at any one time be *in the vicinity of* the operating centre.[6]

(b) the parking arrangements to be provided for authorised vehicles at or in the vicinity of every such operating centre.

In cases where particular difficulties arise or are anticipated in relation to parking, the Licensing Authority will, it is suggested, normally be disposed to attach conditions under this head rather than refuse outright under section 69B(3). The most usual condition is perhaps one prohibiting parking on roads within a given distance

---

[5] Contrast the dictum in Appeal 1984 No W12 *J Cryer & Sons Ltd* that occasional use, even on a regular basis, of another place to park a vehicle overnight will not render that place the vehicle's operating centre if it is *normally* kept elsewhere. See p 45.

[6] Appeal 1986 No X1 *C Smith t/a A1 Demolition*.

from the access to the operating centre, in order to meet objections that the authorised vehicles are 'cluttering up' the approaches to it. It may, however, occasionally be appropriate to have a condition specifying a parking area within the operating centre, for instance in order to distance the parked vehicles from a representor's house;[7] or a condition which aims to control noise etc from parked vehicles. In the *Surrey Heath* v. *NFT* case the Transport Tribunal imposed amongst other things the following condition:

> '(1) The parking arrangements at the operating centre shall be such that while any authorised vehicle is parked there (a) the vehicle's engine is not running except for a period of not exceeding 3 minutes before leaving its parking place or in connection with the maintenance of the vehicles;
> (b) the vehicle's refrigeration unit (if any) is either inoperative or is powered from the mains electricity supply.'

As a means of controlling noise from engines, whether the vehicle's own, or ancillary ones, while the vehicle is stationary, the use of this condition-making power about parking arrangements may be respectfully described as ingenious.

> (c) the times between which there may be carried out at every such operating centre any maintenance, or movement of any authorised vehicle and the times at which any equipment may be used for any such maintenance or movement.

A condition limiting the times of operation and/or maintenance of the authorised vehicles is perhaps the commonest kind of condition imposed as a result of environmental objections and representations. The Licensing Authority has to balance the interests of the applicant for a licence against those of representors whose enjoyment of their land will to some extent be adversely affected by the grant of the licence; as has been seen, the special business interests of the applicant have to be considered where there is no material change. He will in any case have to take all relevant evidence into account, as the Transport Tribunal observed in Appeal 1985 No W7 *Thrapston Warehousing Co Ltd:* 'The Deputy Licensing Authority does not seem to have put the evidence of noise from authorised vehicles in the early morning into the perspective of the undisputed evidence of the number of vehicles using this busy A class road during these hours

---

[7]   As in the condition approved in Appeal 1985 No W4 *R A Nightingale t/a Anglia Fruiterers*.

and the measured noise from them.' On the other hand, a condition prohibiting movement in the very early morning on two days in the week was regarded as acceptable on the basis that the applicant 'will probably find a suitable place or places at which he can leave the vehicle overnight prior to an early start on Wednesday and Saturday mornings.'[8] The Tribunal added: 'Such places would not be operating centres within the definition set out in section 52 of the Transport Act 1982.'

> (d) the means of ingress to and egress from every such operating centre for any authorised vehicle.

The limited meaning of ingress and egress has already been noted (see p 81). While there is no power in the Licensing Authority to control the routeing of vehicles in general, Regulation 21(d) will justify a condition requiring vehicles to turn in one direction only when entering or leaving the operating centre. In Appeal 1986 No X30 *W R Atkinson (Transport) Ltd* the Deputy Licensing Authority had imposed a condition limiting the use by authorised vehicles of certain roads in the vicinity of the operating centre. The Tribunal held that this condition did not fall within any of the categories prescribed in Regulation 21. They said 'Although the noise of authorised vehicles passing to and from an operating centre can be taken into account in determining whether the use of the operating centre will have adverse effects on the environment, that does not permit a condition to be imposed on the use of such roads within the vicinity by authorised vehicles under Regulation 21(d) except at the point of ingress to and egress from the operating centre.'

The Transport Tribunal's statement about their policy of non-interference with conditions imposed by Licensing Authorities except on grounds of law has already been noted (see p 77).

A note on 'undertakings'

In Appeal No Y12 *Mid Suffolk District Council* v. *A Dowell Junior* the Transport Tribunal observed that the effect of undertakings given by applicants in respect of matters for which conditions cannot be imposed may be open to some doubt, and they deprecated the use of undertakings to supply gaps in the legislation. Pending clarification through further appeal cases, the following propositions may be tentatively deduced from the Tribunal's comments and the authority cited in *Dowell:*[9]

---

[8]   Appeal 1985 No W4 *R A Nightingale t/a Anglia Fruiterers.*
[9]   *Regina* v. *Edmonton Licensing Justices Ex Part Baker and Another [1983]* WLR 1000, All ER 545.

(i)   an undertaking extracted or elicited from an applicant at a Public Inquiry would partake of the nature of a condition, and would be enforceable if – and only if – there was power in the Act or Regulations to impose a condition in the same terms;

(ii)   an undertaking volunteered by an applicant might amount to a statement of intention enforceable under section 69(1)(c) of the 1968 Act (see p 103);

(iii)   a voluntary undertaking not amounting to a statement of intention might amount to an assurance which, while not enforceable, could be taken into account in deciding whether or not to grant the licence. If the licence-holder then failed to abide by it, his failure could be relevant on an objection to the renewal of the licence.

It may be added, as the Tribunal pointed out in *Dowell*, that a statement of intention can properly be made only in relation to an application, and has no place in proceedings where the issue is the *continued retention* of an existing licence.[10]

Enforcement of conditions

Breach of any condition properly imposed upon an operator's licence under either section 66 or section 69C is an offence punishable by fine on conviction (see p 85). Breach of a condition imposed by the Licensing Authority under section 66 is also ground for action under section 69, that is to say, the licence involved may be revoked, suspended, curtailed or prematurely terminated.[11] It is also open to the Licensing Authority under section 69(2), in any case in which he has power to give a direction under section 69(1), to attach to the licence any, or any additional, condition of a kind mentioned in section 66. This power is not, it is assumed, a further penalty, but rather to be exercised for the purpose of regulating conduct for the future.

Section 69F makes a breach of condition imposed under section 69C – ie one intended to prevent or minimise adverse effects on environmental conditions – actionable under section 69(1) by revocation, suspension etc of the licence. The effect of section 69F(2)

---

[10] The Licensing Authority should not rely on a statement of intent where the desired result can be achieved by a proper condition: see Appeal 1987 No Y25 *Wessex Construction & Plant Hire Company Ltd.*

[11] The jurisdiction of the Licensing Authority under section 69 is fully dealt with in Chapter 7.

is to add breach of an environmental condition to the grounds available under section 69(1) and to make the other provisions of section 69 applicable to it, eg the right to request a public inquiry under section 69(9) (see further on p 94).

The Transport Tribunal have held that the Licensing Authority cannot remove an operating centre from the licence, even if by reason of a condition not being observed it was found to be no longer suitable. In Appeal 1986 No X9 *J F & A J Trezise t/a John Trezise & Sons* the Tribunal said: 'We do not consider that section 69F of the Act, which gives the Licensing Authority power to revoke, suspend, terminate on a date earlier than that on which it would otherwise expire, or curtail a licence, empowers him to remove an operating centre from a licence.'

CHAPTER 7

The Licensing Authority's Disciplinary Functions

Since the introduction of 'carrier licensing' in 1933, the Licensing Authority has had the power and the duty to monitor the performance of operators of goods vehicles – including those not falling within the scope of the licensing system – and to enforce compliance with the rules governing their proper operation, with particular reference to maintenance of vehicles, weight limits, and drivers' hours regulations. As already stated, he discharges this duty partly by initiating prosecutions for breaches of these rules, a duty which he shares with other enforcement authorities, ie Trading Standards Officers and the police. He has, however, the additional and particular function of controlling the conduct of licensed operators through their licences. The criteria which govern the granting and refusing of applications for licences have already been discussed (pp 13 – 29). The Licensing Authority will also have occasion to exercise the functions peculiar to his jurisdiction of directing the revocation, suspension, curtailment or premature termination of licences and, in special cases, of disqualifying individuals from holding licences or being directors of companies which hold licences.

The nature of the directions which the Licensing Authority is empowered to make, and the grounds on which he may make them, are dealt with in detail below. The powers derive primarily from section 69 of the 1968 Act, and section 69(3) positively requires him, whenever the existence of any of these grounds is brought to his notice in relation to any licence-holder, to consider whether or not to give a direction imposing any one or more of these penalties in respect of that licence. The additional duty and power of the Licensing Authority to revoke a standard licence if the operator ceases to satisfy one or more of the requirements of good repute, appropriate financial standing and professional competence under the Regulations made pursuant to EEC Directive 74/561, are examined separately on pp 108 – 10.

Although the exercise of the powers under section 69 is in practice carried out through the medium of a Public Inquiry at which the operator is invited to state his case – and which indeed he may require as of right[1] – the section as framed envisages that the Licensing Authority, having in his administrative capacity received reports and formed a view about the licence-holder's conduct or performance, may inform him of the order he proposes to make and invite him to say whether he accepts it or wishes an inquiry to be held first. That this is an acceptable procedure under section 69(9) was confirmed in Appeal 1964 No A75 *Anderson Brothers (Westerhope) Ltd* where the Transport Tribunal said that it was not improper to offer a haulier either a short period of suspension or a Public Inquiry, provided that if an inquiry is requested it is conducted with an open mind and in a judicial manner.[2] In the case itself, after hearing the evidence the Licensing Authority imposed a severer penalty than that originally 'offered', and this was upheld by the Tribunal. In practice this procedure is seldom if ever adopted, and proceedings are normally commenced by a 'call-in letter' which sets out the background of the licence, and the matters complained of, and invites the licence-holder to attend a Public Inquiry to show cause why the Licensing Authority should not exercise his powers of revoking, suspending, prematurely terminating or curtailing the licence. Issues not raised in the call-in letter should not be the subject of evidence at the Public Inquiry, at any rate without the agreement of the licence-holder. In Appeal 1972 No J35 *J W H Watson (Rochester) Ltd t/a Olsen Bros* the Tribunal said: 'It was of course perfectly proper for the Licensing Authority to interest himself in the facilities . . . But it seems to us to be wrong to deal with this case on the basis that the appellants had failed to provide proper facilities for the maintenance of their vehicles in the absence of any specific allegation to that effect.' Failure to refer specifically to one of the powers of the Licensing Authority will not, however, prevent the exercise of that power, at any rate if it is a lesser power compared with one specifically referred to. In Appeal 1977 No 01 *J & B J Leddon and F J Drury (t/a Glentrust Demolition and Plant Hire)* the Tribunal said that the failure to include a reference to the power of premature termination did not prevent the Licensing Authority from exercising it, 'since the appellant had notice that they were in jeopardy of having their licence revoked, which would have been a more severe penalty than premature termination'. In particular, if the Licensing Authority has it in mind to consider disqualifying any person, this should be clearly stated in the letter.[3]

---

[1] Section 69(9) provides that no direction in the nature of a penalty under the section may be given without first holding an inquiry if the licence-holder requests one.

[2] See also Appeal 1968 No E40 *John Hill & Sons (Walsall) Ltd.*

[3] Appeal 1984 No V9 *I C Ireland.*

It will be appreciated that the number of convictions of licensed operators, and prohibitions of their vehicles – the principal grounds for a direction under section 69 – is considerable in any given period, and although all must be considered (section 69(3)), comparatively few are made the subject of a direction, since the number of Public Inquiries which can be held in a given period is limited by considerations of cost and availability of staff; this in turn determines the threshold of seriousness which is considered to justify a direction being given. The majority are dealt with, after due consideration, by the issue to the operator of a 'warning letter' drawing his attention to the rules governing the matter in question, and warning that any repetition would be likely to lead to a sterner action being taken by the Licensing Authority. The issue of a 'warning letter' is noted on the operator's record.

The effect on a licence-holder's business of a direction under section 69, especially if it entails revocation or suspension of the licence, is obviously potentially very great, and the Transport Tribunal have more than once stated that every call-in letter should include a recommendation that the licence-holder should seek informed advice;[4] but there is no rule that a licence should not be revoked if the holder is not legally represented, provided due warning is given.[5]

The Licensing Authority has no power to summon an operator before him, or to require his attendance at an inquiry. It is possible, however, that the High Court on an application to that end might issue a subpoena to compel the attendances of witnesses before him. In *Currie* v. *Chief Constable of Surrey* [1982] 1 WLR 89 Mr Justice McNeill said that this could be done where the inferior court or tribunal (a) is recognised by law, (b) acts judicially or quasi-judicially in the exercise of its functions, (c) acts on evidence, whether or not on oath, and (d) has no or no sufficient power of its own to secure the attendance of witnesses or the production of documents. All these conditions seem to be satisfied in respect of a Licensing Authority. Be that as it may, the call-in letter will often contain a warning that if the licence-holder does not attend, a decision may be made in his absence; in some Traffic Areas this warning may not be given until the licence-holder has failed to attend one inquiry and is being 'called' to a second. If a licence-holder does not appear at an inquiry the Licensing Authority will normally wish to be satisfied that the call-in letter was received by the licence-holder, before giving a

---

[4]   Appeal 1982 No T11 *M Dyer & A W H Cork (t/a M & B Transport)*;
       Appeal 1984 No V4 *D W Briggs (Plant Hire) Ltd.*
[5]   Appeal 1985 No W3 *Herbert Morrison.*

direction in his absence. The foregoing applies equally to proceedings pursuant to Regulation 9 of the 1984 Regulations (SI No 176) with the distinction, already referred to (p 32; and see p 108), that on a strict interpretation of the relevant regulation, revocation may be ordered on a summary basis.

Grounds for action under section 69

Action under section 69 in respect of an operator's licence may be taken only by the Licensing Authority who granted the licence. The grounds on which he may direct the revocation, suspension, premature termination or curtailment of the licence may be placed under seven heads:

- (i) breach of a condition of the licence: s.69(1)(a);
- (ii) 'relevant convictions': s.69(1)(b)(i) and (ii);
- (iii) prohibitions: s.69(1)(b)(i);
- (iv) false statements of fact and unfulfilled statements of intention: s.69(1)(c);
- (v) bankruptcy or liquidation: s.69(1)(d);
- (vi) material change of circumstances: s.69(1)(e);
- (vii) breach of disqualification order: s.69(1)(f).

These grounds may vary in importance and frequency of application. They are examined in more detail below.

Section 69(1)(a)

'That the licence-holder has contravened any condition attached to his licence under section 66.'

As has been seen, the scope of conditions which may be imposed under section 66 is somewhat limited, but the condition most likely to be enforced under section 69(1)(a) is one requiring convictions to be reported. A 'charge' under this head would not perhaps be made on its own, but would be linked with one under section 69(1)(b) alleging the conviction itself. If a condition requiring the reporting of convictions has been attached to the licence, this will call for the reporting of all convictions including those consequent upon prosecutions brought by the Licensing Authority himself.

Section 69(1)(b)(i) and (ii)

'That during the five years ending with the date on which the direction is given there has been:

(i) any such conviction as is mentioned in subsection 4(a) to (f);[6]

(ii) convictions of the kind mentioned in subsection 4(g) which the Licensing Authority considers to be sufficiently numerous to justify action by him.'

With regard to (ii), convictions under subsection (4)(g) relate to contraventions by the licence-holder, his servants or agents, of parking restriction orders, or lorry routeing provisions under Road Traffic Regulation Acts. No information is available as to how many convictions a Licensing Authority would regard as sufficiently numerous; and in the absence of any system for such convictions to be reported (other than by the licence-holder himself) it is safe to say that this particular ground under paragraph (b)(ii) is seldom if ever invoked.

Relevant Convictions

The convictions which can lead to the giving of a direction under section 69(1), and which are generally referred to in the Act and Regulations as 'relevant' or 'specified' convictions, are as follows:

1. A conviction, in relation to a goods vehicle, of the licence-holder or a servant or agent of his, relating to:

(i) the maintenance of vehicles in a fit and serviceable condition;

(ii) exceeding speed limits, overloading and improper loading of vehicles;

(iii) the licensing of drivers.

'Goods vehicle' means any motor vehicle constructed or adapted for the carriage of goods, and not only one for which an operator's licence is required.

2. A conviction of the licence-holder for:

(i) contravention of the licensing provisions of the Act, ie essentially for using a goods vehicle on a road otherwise than under the authority of an operator's licence duly granted and valid at the relevant time. This would include using a vehicle which, although within the total number of vehicles authorised by the

---

[6] ie 'relevant' or 'specified' convictions.

        licence, was not specified therein pursuant to section 61(1)(a) – unless it had not then been in the operator's possession for at least one month.[7]

  (ii) forging of licences or other identification documents, or the making of false statements for the purpose of obtaining a licence, or preventing the grant or variation of a licence. (Road Traffic Act 1960 sections 233 and 235.)

  (iii) contravention of any regulations made under s.91 of the Act which are prescribed for the purposes of subsection 69(4)(b)(iii). While many regulations have been made under the Act, none of them has, it seems, been prescribed under this subsection, which must therefore be considered to be non-operative for the time being.

3. A conviction of the licence-holder or a servant or agent of his for contravening (or conspiring to contravene) the law as to the limitation on drivers' hours and the keeping of records thereof, whether manually or by the use of tachographs.

4. A conviction of the licence-holder for contravening (or conspiring to contravene) section 200 of the Customs and Excise Act 1952 dealing with unlawful use of rebated fuel oil.

5. A conviction of the holder of the licence or a servant or agent of his, in relation to an international road haulage permit within the meaning of the Road Traffic Act 1972, of sections 169 or 170 of that Act, which relate to forgery or alterations of permits, or false statements made in order to obtain permits.

6. A conviction of the holder of the licence or a servant or agent of his under section 2 of the International Road Haulage Permits Act 1975, for the offence of removing a goods vehicle from the United Kingdom when it is under prohibition because of failure to carry or produce a valid permit.

7. A conviction of the holder of the licence under section 18 of the Road Safety Act 1967, or section 59 of the Road Traffic Act 1972.

The sections referred to in paragraph 7 empower the Secretary of State to make Regulations requiring operators to inspect their vehicles and to keep records of such inspections. No Regulations have so far been made under these provisions, but failure to inspect the licensed vehicles and to keep records of such inspections would of course be a breach of the undertaking entered into on application, and this would be a ground for action under section 69(1)(c) dealt with below.

---

[7] see p 12.

8. A conviction of the holder of the licence of an offence under Regulation 33(2) of the Goods Vehicles (Operators' Licences, Qualifications and Fees) Regulations 1984, SI 1984 No 176.

9. A conviction of the holder of the licence of an offence under Regulation 33(3) of the 1984 Regulations.

These two paragraphs make it an offence, first, to use a goods vehicle under a restricted licence for carrying goods for hire or reward; and secondly, for using a standard national licence for carrying goods for hire or reward on international transport operations. While any conviction under either provision is a ground for a direction under the section, section 69(3A), inserted by the Road Traffic Act 1974, makes it mandatory for the Licensing Authority, if there is a second conviction under Regulation 33(2) within 5 years of a first, to order the revocation of the licence.

Note: It will be noted that in respect of some of the convictions listed as relevant, the conviction must be of the licence-holder, whether individual, partnership or company, while in others the conviction of a servant or agent will also give grounds for action against the licence.

Notice of Convictions

Apart from convictions resulting from prosecution by the Licensing Authority himself – of which he may reasonably be assumed to be aware – he must rely for information about convictions on notification by the other enforcement agencies in the field, namely the police and County Trading Standards Officers. Magistrates' Courts do not automatically advise Licensing Authorities of relevant convictions, although if the Traffic Area receives notice from other sources (eg from reports in the press), the courts will supply details of particular convictions on request. Some Trading Standards departments regularly supply returns of convictions – mainly for overloading offences – but there is no obligation to do so and practices vary. The police do not normally supply information about convictions unless they are objecting to applications on grounds of fitness or good repute. The difficulties encountered by Licensing Authorities in their attempts to secure regular reporting to them of relevant convictions of licensed operators and their drivers have been the subject of recurrent comment in the annual reports submitted by them to the Secretary of State.

No other convictions, other than those listed in paragraphs 1 to 9 above, are 'relevant', ie grounds for proceeding against the licence under section 69, although as has been seen (p 00), convictions for fraud or dishonest behaviour generally can amount to conduct which will deprive a licence-holder of his 'good repute', and thus make the licence liable to revocation under Regulation 9 of the 1984 Regulations.

Prohibitions

The second part of section 69(1)(b)(i) refers to prohibitions under subsection (4)(h), that is to say either a prohibition of the use of a vehicle under section 57 of the Road Traffic Act 1972 on the grounds of defects causing it to be unroadworthy (commonly called a 'GV9'); or a prohibition of the driving of a vehicle which has been found to be overweight (GV160). In either case the licence-holder must have been the owner of the vehicle when the prohibition was imposed, that is to say, it must either belong to him, or be in his possession under an agreement for hire purchase, hire or loan. This rule was applied in Appeal 1973 No K4 *V Davies t/a Jubilee Transport*, when the Transport Tribunal observed: 'The vehicle which was the subject of the prohibition was not specified on the appellant's licence and the appellant stated in evidence that, though he was proposing to buy the vehicle, it still belonged to the vendor when the prohibition was issued. If this was true, the prohibition was not such a one as mentioned in s.69(4)(h) of the Transport Act 1968 and therefore could not form the basis of proceedings under s.69(1)(b)(i).'

The power to prohibit vehicles for unroadworthiness, and for overloading, is not limited to those which are subject to operator licensing; an operator's licence may therefore be at risk under section 69(4)(h) if any of his vehicles which are constructed or adapted for the carriage of goods are the subject of a prohibition. Normally, however, a licence-holder will not be made the subject of proceedings under section 69 unless one or more of his authorised vehicles have been prohibited.

'GV9s': The imposition of a GV9 on a vehicle by a Vehicle Examiner prohibits the use of the vehicle on a road until it is lifted or 'cleared' after a further inspection by the same or different Vehicle Examiner. A prohibition may be imposed with a direction making it irremoveable unless and until the vehicle is presented for clearance at a Heavy Goods Vehicle Testing Station (Transport Act 1978 amending the Road Traffic Act 1972). A GV9 may be 'immediate' or 'delayed'; it will have effect immediately if any of the defects recorded by the Vehicle Examiner are in his judgment likely to make use of the vehicle a source of immediate danger to the public. If none of the defects is of this nature, but there are defects which if not remedied will soon become a source of danger, the prohibition may be delayed for up to ten days. If all the defects have not been cleared by the date stated on the GV9, the prohibition will then come into effect.

The defects for which a prohibition must or should be imposed, and whether it should be 'immediate' or 'delayed', are set out in detail in the *Testers' Manual*, which constitutes in effect a code of practice for vehicle examiners and testers nationally. Thus while there is obviously room for differences of opinion between examiners about the seriousness of any given defect, such differences can only be marginal. The recipient of the prohibition has the right to request a second inspection by a Certifying Officer[8] if he disagrees with the examiner's judgment and consequent decision; the vehicle meanwhile has to be left unused in its existing state, and for this reason advantage is seldom taken of this right of appeal. It is an offence under s.57(9)(a) of the Road Traffic Act 1972 to use a vehicle on a road while it is under effective prohibition.

Subject to the operator's right to challenge the prohibition by requesting an inspection by a Certifying Officer, a GV9 'speaks for itself'[9] and the Licensing Authority may take it into account and give a direction under section 69(1) without evidence from the Vehicle Examiner who imposed it[10]; but he will not normally do this if the operator wishes to contest the prohibition and/or cross-examine the Vehicle Examiner. In other words, the GV9 itself raises a *prima facie* case against the operator, which he may seek to oppose. A Vehicle Examiner will not, however, be allowed to give evidence of matters contained in a report by a colleague, of which he has no personal knowledge, at any rate unless the contents are accepted by the licence-holder as correct. In Appeal 1981 No S9 *Joseph Torok t/a K & J Plant & Tipper Hire* the Transport Tribunal said: 'If reliance is to be placed by a Licensing Authority acting in his judicial capacity upon a report produced to him in his administrative capacity[11] . . . the report should be produced and evidence should be given by the person who made the report . . . We have therefore decided to ignore Mr S's "evidence" and to found our decision on the prohibitions and the evidence given by the appellant.'

---

[8] a professional officer, usually an Assistant Mechanical Engineer on the staff of the Licensing Authority.

[9] Appeal 1976 No N18 *Benjamin Wragg*.

[10] See Appeal 1966 No C12 *Transport Holding Company*.

[11] The report was not produced at the Inquiry, but was sent to the Transport Tribunal with other documents. The Vehicle Examiner (Mr S) gave 'evidence' taken verbatim from this report prepared by a colleague who was not called.

There is no rule corresponding to section 178(4) of the Road Traffic Act 1960, since repealed, which required the Licensing Authority, before giving a direction as to revocation, suspension etc, to be satisfied that prohibitions or convictions were so frequent, or the acts leading up to them so wilful, or the danger to the public so evident, that such a direction ought to be given. Naturally the decision of the Licensing Authority will depend, for its severity or otherwise, on the seriousness of the offence and the previous record of the licence-holder in that regard (see pp 111 – 12).

'GV160': A Traffic Examiner, or other duly authorised enforcement officer, who has found a vehicle to be overweight by more than statutorily permitted tolerance (if any) may prohibit its movement on the road until the weight has been reduced or, in the case of axle overload only, readjusted. In nearly all instances of overloading the licence-holder – and perhaps the driver also – will be liable to prosecution for the offence in the magistrates' court having jurisdiction over the area where the weighing took place, whether or not the vehicle is also prohibited.

The respective merits, from an enforcement point of view, of prohibition and prosecution, have sometimes been debated. It is clearly desirable, on principle, that persons committing offences should be brought before the courts, and the question has usually been whether the offender should be prohibited as well as prosecuted. Prohibition, besides involving the operator in the trouble and expense of offloading and perhaps arranging for a relief vehicle, has the advantage of preventing the first vehicle from continuing (for the time being at least) to be a source of possible damage to roads and bridges, or of possible danger to other road users by reason of excess weight. Licence-holders convicted of overloading offences will probably be called before the appropriate Licensing Authority primarily because of the conviction, and the prohibition may be combined with the conviction for the purposes of section 69. Offenders who do not hold operators' licences – eg operators of foreign vehicles – do not of course come within the Licensing Authority's personal jurisdiction at all, although his enforcement staff may take action through the courts under the Road Traffic (Foreign Vehicles) Act 1972.

It will have been noted that for action under section 69(1)(b) to be taken, the convictions or prohibitions must have been incurred or been imposed, respectively, within the 5 years ending with the date on which the direction is given, and not – if the licence-holder is being called to a Public Inquiry – with the date of the call-in letter. Since the maximum duration of a licence is 5 years, convictions and prohibitions incurred towards the beginning of the 5-year period will probably have preceded the grant of the current licence and may perhaps be considered to have been condoned by that grant, unless indeed they had been concealed from the Licensing Authority by the applicant.

Section 69(1)(c) to (f)

These four paragraphs set out the grounds other than breach of conditions, convictions and prohibitions, on which the Licensing Authority may base a direction to revoke, suspend, prematurely terminate or curtail a licence.

Paragraph (c)

'that the holder of the licence made for the purposes of his application . . . a statement of fact which (whether to his knowledge or not) was false or a statement of intention or expectation which has not been fulfilled.'

Statements of fact and intention or expectation may be made in the Application Forms GV79 or GV81 (in respect of variations) or by letter, or verbally at the hearing of an application. Statements of *fact* in the application form relate to four principal issues:

(i) the identity and previous experience of any existing transport manager, or other person, eg the applicant or a partner, put forward as 'professionally competent';

(ii) previous convictions of the applicant, whether an individual, a company or a partnership, and/or of the nominated transport manager;

(iii) whether the applicant, or his partners or directors (if a company) have ever been put into bankruptcy or liquidation, or disqualified from managing a company;

(iv) the existing financial resources of the applicant.

Licensing Authorities will not normally accept an application unless these questions are answered.

Statements of *intention* are primarily those set out in the declaration which forms part of the application signed by the applicant, in the following terms:

'I will make proper arrangements so that:
- the rules on drivers' hours are observed and proper records are kept;
- vehicles are not overloaded;
- vehicles are kept fit and serviceable;

- drivers will report safety faults in vehicles as soon as possible;
- records are kept (for 15 months) of all safety inspections, routine maintenance and repairs to vehicles, and make these available on request.

I will

- have adequate financial resources to maintain the vehicles covered by the licence;
- tell the Licensing Authority of any changes or convictions which affect the licence;
- maintain adequate financial resources for the administration of the business.' [Applies to standard applicants only.]

These statements of intention are very comprehensive, and reinforce and duplicate many of the specific provisions already dealt with – and indeed at least one of those yet to be covered, namely that relating to a standard licence holder ceasing to be of 'appropriate financial standing'. It is customary to include in 'call-in letters', along with statements as to convictions for overloading, GV9 prohibitions etc, a charge that the appropriate statement of intention has not been fulfilled. It may be noted that the application form does not call for a specific undertaking that vehicles will be inspected at regular intervals of time or mileage. However, the applicant does undertake to 'make proper arrangements' to keep the vehicles fit and serviceable, and such arrangements would include vehicle checks and safety inspections as advised in Appendix 5 of the Department of Transport's publication *A Guide to Goods Vehicle Operator Licensing* (GV74). GV9 prohibitions, and/or convictions for breach of Construction and Use Regulations, may themselves be evidence of failure to fulfil statements of intention about maintenance; in addition, Vehicle Examiners may give evidence of the result of their inspection of the premises, vehicles, records and systems of the operator. The reports of Vehicle Examiners on their inspections are normally made available to the Licensing Authority – and may indeed be the basis of the decision to consider section 69 action – but at a Public Inquiry the Licensing Authority will take into account only of those parts of it which are given orally in evidence by the Vehicle Examiner.[12]

Failure to fulfil a statement of intention may exceptionally stand alone, as exemplified in Appeal 1979 No Q9 *H W Dines & Co Ltd* v. *Cherwell District Council*, where a question arose as to the location of the applicant's operating centre. The Transport Tribunal pointed

---

[12] See Appeal 1981 No S9 *Joseph Torok t/a K & J Plant & Tipper Hire*.

out that the proposed location of an operating centre was a matter of intention, and continued: 'If the appellants were to be granted a licence and continued not to have their operating centre located at Merton, they would lay themselves open to proceedings under section 69 of the Act of 1968 on the ground that they had made for the purposes of their amended application a statement of intention which had not been fulfilled.'

A particular application of alleged breach of a statement of intention was seen in Appeal 1984 No V14 *Gordon Wright*. The operator's drivers were 'self-employed' for tax and national insurance purposes. The Licensing Authority took the view that in these circumstances the operator could not fulfil his statement of intention that he would ensure that the rules on drivers' hours were observed, because he could not exercise sufficient control. The Tribunal held that the drivers were sufficiently under the control of the operator for his statutory obligation to be discharged and his statement of intention to be accordingly fulfilled. In effect the Licensing Authority was seeking, and obtained, the Tribunal's ruling on whether 'self-employed' drivers were 'employee drivers' within section 95(3)(a) of the Act.

Paragraph (d)

'that the holder of the licence has been adjudicated bankrupt or, where the holder is a company, has gone into liquidation (not being a voluntary liquidation for the purpose of reconstruction).'

It appears from this provision that the scheme of the 1968 Act was that an operator who was made bankrupt or, being a company, went or was put into liquidation, did not automatically cease to be licensed. No doubt in most cases he would in practice cease operations and surrender the licence; but if he did not, it remained a matter for the Licensing Authority's discretion whether to revoke the licence. The position is still the same in respect of restricted licences, but different rules apply for standard licences, as will be seen. In Appeal 1980 No R2 *Trevor Beacock (t/a M and R Haulage)* the Transport Tribunal said: 'In considering this matter it is necessary to have in mind that action taken under s.69(1)(d) of the Act of 1968 with regard to a licence of which the holder has been adjudicated bankrupt differs from action taken under the other provisions of s.69(1) in that it is not a penalty for past shortcomings on the part of the holder of the licence, and that it is therefore inappropriate to look for either aggravating or mitigating circumstances. All that has to be considered is whether it is consistent with the purposes of the Act of 1968 that a person who has been adjudicated bankrupt should continue to hold an operator's licence. . . . In our view, revocation is *prima facie* the right course for a Licensing Authority to take upon the bankruptcy of the holder of an operator's licence. Some lesser action is legally permissible and may be justifiable if the circumstances of a case warrant it . . . .'

It is not a ground for revocation of the licence that the principal manager of the business is an undischarged bankrupt, even if he is to all intents and purposes the actual operator. In Appeal 1980 No R9 *BH Transport*, the Transport Tribunal said: 'Although the holder of an operator's licence, the appellant is not personally engaged in the running of the business. The business is run by her husband, and the only reason why the appellant is the licensee is that her husband is an undischarged bankrupt. The Deputy Licensing Authority took a somewhat unfavourable view of this state of affairs. It does not, however, appear to us that it is a *sine qua non* of holding an operator's licence that the licensee should be personally engaged in the running of the business. It is quite permissible for a licensee to have no more than a financial interest in the business, provided that he or she employs competent persons to ensure that there is proper compliance with the relevant legislation, though in such circumstances the licensee cannot seek to evade his or her personal responsibility for any failure to comply with the legislation.'

This last principle is of course of general application, and not only in the context of bankruptcy.

One difficulty facing the Licensing Authority is to know that a person or company is bankrupt or in liquidation. In the *Trevor Beacock* case the Licensing Authority did not discover the true facts for some 6 years. There is no system for the Courts or Official Receivers to advise the Licensing Authority of such cases. The consequenes may not be legally embarrassing in the case of restricted licences, to which the principle in *BH Transport* applies, and revocation is discretionary. As will be seen, however, it is very different in relation to standard licences, which (subject to certain procedures whose effect is retrospective) automatically become invalid, and may give rise to problems for that reason.

Paragraph (e)

' . . . that there has been since the licence was granted or varied a material change in any of the circumstances of the holder of the licence which were relevant to the grant or variation of the licence.'

This ground will be available to the Licensing Authority in any case in which, if the circumstances of the applicant resulting from the material change had existed at the date of the application, it would or might have been refused. In most cases the events or acts constituting the material change will be actionable under a different head, eg if the licence-holder has had convictions, or if his financial situation has significantly altered, the sections relating to those particular matters would be available. However, there may well be cases in relation to restricted licences where it is alleged that the licence-holder has ceased to be a 'fit person' on grounds other than specific relevant convictions. The language of the paragraph appears to confine the material change to matters affecting the licence-holder personally (or, if a company, affecting its directors or officers) rather than circumstances extraneous to him, eg the identity or suitability of an operating centre. However, in Appeal 1982 No T10 *Stone Corner Hauliers Ltd* it was not disputed at the Public Inquiry and was conceded before the Tribunal that the change of operating centre from that which the applicants had originally stated they intended to use was a material change in 'the circumstances of the licence-holder' within the section. It seems at least doubtful whether, had the proposition been contested, the Tribunal would have so decided, and it is suggested that the case is not an authority for its validity.[13]

Paragraph (f)

> 'that the licence is liable to revocation, suspension, premature termination or curtailment by virtue of a direction under subsection (6) of this section.'

The ground stated in this paragraph is consequential on subsections (5) and (6) of section 69. Subsection (5) empowers the Licensing Authority, in cases where he revokes an operator's licence, to disqualify the holder (or if the holder is a company or a partnership, any director or partner) from holding or obtaining an operator's licence, indefinitely or for a fixed period. Under subsection (6) he may direct that if while such disqualification is in force the disqualified person controls, or is a director of, a company, or is a member of a partnership, which holds an operator's licence, the licence in question shall be liable to revocation etc. Paragraph (f) supplies the power to carry that threat into execution.[14]

---

[13] cf Appeal 1979 No Q9 *H W Dines & Co Ltd* v. *Cherwell District Council* (see p 104) where a similar change of operating centre was said to be referrable to the nonfulfilment of a statement of intention.

[14] There is no power to disqualify a director of a company from holding a licence unless the licence of that company has first been revoked: Appeal 1987 No Y37 *D F C International Ltd, D F Collision and J M Collision.*

Sanctions under the 1984 Regulations (Standard Licences)

Regulation 9(1) of the Goods Vehicles (Operators' Licences, Qualifications and Fees) Regulations 1984 provide as follows: 'Subject to the provisions of paragraphs (2) and (4) a Licensing Authority by whom a licence was granted shall revoke the licence if it appears to that authority at any time that the holder no longer satisfies the requirement to be of good repute, the requirement to be of appropriate financial standing or the requirement as to professional competence.' Paragraph (4), as substituted by the Amendment Regulations 1987 (SI 1987 No 841), provides that a direction given by a Licensing Authority under paragraph (1) shall be regarded as having been given under section 69(1), so that the various other provisions of section 69 (except subsection (3)) apply, eg as to the right to have a Public Inquiry and the right of appeal under section 70.

It will be noted that once 'it appears' to the Licensing Authority that one or more of the requirements are not satisfied, revocation is mandatory. So far as good repute and financial standing are concerned, therefore, Licensing Authorities will normally elect to proceed under section 69, unless the case is so serious that revocation must be considered in any event. What constitutes good repute and appropriate financial standing has already been considered (see pp 29 – 39). No rules can be laid down as to what conduct would cause good repute to be lost, or what evidence would be sufficient to prove loss of appropriate financial standing. Paragraph 9(2) requires the Licensing Authority, before ordering revocation, to give notice in writing to the licence-holder that he is considering doing so, stating the grounds, and informing the holder that he may make written representations within 21 days, 'and the Licensing Authority shall consider all such representations duly made'. Paragraph 9(4) applies to any revocation order made under paragraph 9(1) the right of appeal provided by section 70(1) of the Act. There is no record of any appeal from a revocation as a result of written representations alone, and it is perhaps unlikely that many such orders have been made. In practice Licensing Authorities will either deal with the matter at Public Inquiry under the general discretion to do so given them by section 87(1) of the 1968 Act, or will combine charges under regulation 9 with others arising under section 69, so that the option of a lesser penalty than revocation is retained, and call the licence-holder to a Public Inquiry under procedures discussed in Chapter 8.

An example of the first kind of proceeding is Appeal 1985 No W3 *Herbert Morrison*. The Licensing Authority invited the licence-holder to attend a Public Inquiry at which he would consider revocation on grounds of loss of both good repute and appropriate financial standing, without any alternative grounds under section 69. The Tribunal upheld the revocation on the 'good repute' ground. It seems that where the Licensing Authority has 'plumped' for Regulation 9 proceedings, with the choice of 'revocation or nothing', he cannot give a lesser direction – eg suspension or curtailment – on section 69 grounds, unless indeed an amendment of the 'summons' to include such grounds were proposed in the course of the proceedings and accepted without objection by the licence-holder.

It is equally a ground for mandatory revocation under paragraph 9 that the licence-holder no longer has the necessary professional competence, probably because the person fulfilling that requirement has left his employment. The difference in this case is that it is not a matter of judgment but of fact whether the requirement as to professional competence is satisfied or not. There would therefore appear to be little or nothing that a licence-holder could offer by way of representations under paragraph 9(2). However, whether for this reason or otherwise, Regulation 10 provides a separate code to cover loss of professional competence (amongst other things: it also covers bankruptcy, liquidation and lunacy).

Paragraph 10(1) provides that where the requirement of professional competence ceases to be satisfied in relation to a standard licence, the licence 'shall cease to have effect', save as provided in sub-paragraph (6)(b). The latter provides that the Licensing Authority shall not be required to revoke the licence for such period, up to a maximum of 18 months, as he may determine. The reference to a requirement to revoke presumably relates back to paragraph 9(1), since under paragraph 10 the licence simply ceases to have effect. There is clearly a lack of harmony between the two paragraphs, with two procedures running somewhat uneasily side by side. In practice Licensing Authorities tend to combine the two, and give notice that they propose to revoke the licence, but grant a period of time for a qualified person to be employed, or for an individual director, partner or employee to take and pass the examination, as may be appropriate.

The automatic invalidation of the licence by paragraph 10 tends to cause greater difficulties in cases of bankruptcy and liquidation. As already stated, it not infrequently happens that an individual becomes bankrupt, or a company goes into liquidation, without informing the Licensing Authority and without ceasing to operate vehicles under their licence. Regulation 10(6)(a) provides a procedure whereby, provided timely notice is given to the Licensing Authority, the licence may continue in force for the benefit of another person who has in fact taken over the trade or business in question, and who applies for a new licence: such other person being then deemed to be the holder of the (otherwise invalidated) licence until his application for a new licence is disposed of.

If the provisions of paragraph 10(6) are not invoked – and they seldom if ever are – the licence remains of no effect, and therefore any operations by the bankrupt or company in liquidation are unauthorised, whether the facts are known to the Licensing Authority or not. If and when they do become known to him, he will strictly be bound to treat the licence as ineffective and the operator as being in breach of the law. In the case of *Trevor Beacock* referred to above, the Licensing Authority had renewed the licence when the operator was already bankrupt, and on discovery revoked the licence under section 69(1)(d).

CHAPTER 8

Exercise of Powers Under Section 69

Before considering these powers in detail it will be appropriate to discuss the philosophy behind the jurisdiction of the Licensing Authority in exercising these functions. In Appeal 1966 No C12 *Transport Holding Company* the Transport Tribunal considered the nature of a Public Inquiry under what is now section 69 of the 1968 Act. They said: 'Such an inquiry is not like the trial of a criminal charge, where the onus of proving the case is upon the prosecution. Here there is no prosecutor. It is the Licensing Authority himself who initiates the proceedings. Clearly he is not going to do that unless he considers that there is a *prima facie* case for so doing. He is not under any obligation to hold a Public Inquiry unless the holder of the licence requests him to do so under [section 69(9)] of the Act. The function of the inquiry, as we see it, is to give the holder of the licence an opportunity of showing cause why the Licensing Authority should not give the direction which he has in mind to give. The Licensing Authority must obviously disclose to the holder of the licence at or before the inquiry the information on which he is minded to act, so that the holder of the licence can direct his arguments aright, but if the Licensing Authority does this, he does all that natural justice requires of him.'

The Licensing Authority will frequently be giving directions relating to the licence as a result of one or more convictions of the licence-holder, eg for overloading, bad maintenance or breaches of drivers' hours and records rules. It is sometimes argued that any penalty imposed affecting the licence represents a second punishment for the same offence, and thus amounts to 'double jeopardy'. The argument is untenable (a) on strictly legal grounds, because the legislation clearly makes the fact of conviction a ground for a direction in the nature of a penalty affecting the licence, and (b) on the more general basis that the Licensing Authority's jurisdiction corresponds to that of the disciplinary body of a professional association acting with the object of maintaining standards, and removing those members of it whose activities bring the profession or calling into disrepute.

The argument is also sometimes heard that, because the Licensing Authority exercises his powers in order to safeguard the public, his primary concern should be to ensure that licence-holders will operate safely and efficiently in the future, and that he should not give directions as penalties, whether to punish for past shortcomings, or as a deterrent to others. It is however very well settled, by Transport Tribunal decisions too numerous to list, that directions under section 69 are in reality, and are intended to be, penalties, and are properly so described.[1] To take one case as representative of many, in Appeal 1968 No E36 *Page & Co (Contractors) Ltd* the Tribunal said: 'It seems to us that the Licensing Authority was right in imposing a penalty. Even if one accepts that the appellants have taken steps to mend their ways, nevertheless one cannot regard repentance as absolving an offender altogether from paying for his previous offences. It has to be borne in mind that the object of the jurisdiction being exercised by the Licensing Authority is not only to punish offenders for their faults in the past, but also to deter others from doing likewise in the future.' In Appeal 1974 No L9 *Supertow Services Ltd* the Tribunal said: 'The proper approach under [section 69] is to have regard to the matters of which notice has been given to the licence-holder and then to decide what, if any, is the appropriate penalty to be imposed.' This dictum was cited in a Scottish appeal 1974 No L37 *George Sutherland t/a Express Deliveries*, in which the appellant relied on *Robinson* v. *Secretary of State for the Environment* [1973] 1WLR 1139 for the proposition that the Licensing Authority should look to the future and not aim to impose penalties. That case was, however, decided on the very different provisions of section 127(7) of the Road Traffic Act 1960 relating to public service vehicle licences, since repealed and replaced by a system of operators' licensing similar to that for goods vehicles.

Naturally the severity of the penalty depends on all the circumstances of the case, and perhaps the majority of appeals to the Transport Tribunal from 'disciplinary' decisions of Licensing Authority have concerned the appropriateness of the penalty imposed. In Appeal 1974 No L35 *Stansted Container Service Ltd* the Transport Tribunal observed: 'Matters of penalty are always difficult. Different people can take different views of what is adequate or inadequate, but an Appellate Court such as this ought to

---

[1] The principle was stated in *R Hampton & Sons* (1964) 32 Traffic cases, on p281, where the Court of Appeal said that action under SI78 of the Act (ie the Road Traffic Act 1960) dealing with revocation, suspension and curtailment of carriers licences, 'is taken for the purpose of punishing the offender and is bound to act as a deterrent'.

be slow to interfere with a decision of an original tribunal on the matter of penalty unless there is something wrong with it in principle.'

The underlying objects of the Act are nevertheless in the last resort more important than penalties, as the Tribunal observed in Appeal 1976 No N10 *Gairloch Construction Ltd:* 'We agree with Mr McGhie's submission that to ensure road safety in the future is of greater importance than to punish the appellants for their previous shortcomings.'

The directions which the Licensing Authority may give are set out in section 69(1) of the 1968 Act. On grounds listed in the section, and discussed on p 96, he may direct that the licence be revoked, suspended, terminated on a date earlier than that on which it would otherwise expire, or curtailed. The provision relating to 'premature termination' was inscrtcd by the Road Traffic Act 1974 to take its place between suspension and curtailment. If the penalties were – as appears to be the case – intended to be listed in descending order of severity, premature termination should perhaps have followed rather than preceded curtailment, as it involves the licence-holder only in having to make an application for a fresh licence earlier than he would otherwise have done;[2] however, this direction can be and frequently is combined with an order for suspension or curtailment.

The directions considered

Revocation

This is the ultimate penalty, and is comparatively seldom imposed, and hardly ever on a first appearance before the Licensing Authority. The kind of conduct which would lead to revocation would be such as would make the licence-holder not a fit person to hold a licence. This could well be so serious as to justify immediate revocation,[3] but the more common case is one in which, after warnings and one or two cases of curtailment or suspension, no alternative to revocation is left. A typical case of this kind is Appeal 1981 No S11 *William North Curtis*, where the Transport Tribunal concluded their judgment in these terms: 'Having regard to all the circumstances of this case, we are of opinion that the proper penalty is revocation and that it would be unsafe to allow the appellant to continue to operate until he is in a

---

[2]   The fees applicable to any full twelve months of the 'unexpired portion' of a suspended or prematurely terminated licence are refundable: see Goods Vehicles (Operators' Licences, Qualifications and Fees)(Amendment) Regulations 1987, SI 1987 No.84l.

[3]   As in Appeal 1982 No T2 *S I S Chemicals Ltd.*

position to satisfy the Licensing Authority that he will be conducting his business in a satisfactory manner.[4]

It is not possible to extract from the cases any absolute rule as to when revocation of the licence – other than in cases where revocation is mandatory, eg loss of professional competence – is necessary or justified. It may, however, be helpful to set out by way of illustration a number of recent appeals where directions for the revocation of the licence have been considered:

1985 No W10:   failure to keep records of maintenance, prohibition (GV9), failure to attend inquiry. Appeal dismissed.

1985 No W18:   convictions for offences including false declarations, fraudulent use of exercise licence, use of prohibited vehicle. Ten GV9s over 3 years. Dismissed.

1985 NoW24:   failure to maintain, prohibitions, failure to attend inquiry. Revocation of continuing licence and refusal of renewal upheld.

1986 No X2:   numerous convictions for overloading and breaches of drivers' hours and records regulations. Revocation and one month's disqualification of directors upheld.

1987 No Y6:   conviction of managing director for serious offences, large fine and suspended prison sentence; revocation of company's licence upheld.

Unless the licence-holder is disqualified under section 69(5) from holding or applying for a licence, he may always apply for a fresh licence and seek to persuade the Licensing Authority that the shortcomings which led to the revocation have been corrected. It is not uncommon for a Licensing Authority, having either revoked or refused to renew or vary a licence, to indicate a period after which he might favourably consider a fresh application. Although this is done primarily to assist the licence-holder, there is no jurisdiction to give such an indication, as the Transport Tribunal pointed out in Appeal 1986 No X28 *Kenneth Harry Moorhead*. The Licensing Authority had refused an application to increase the number of vehicles, and added that the applicant would have to show 'in the following year' that he could maintain his vehicles properly. The Tribunal, after dismissing the appeal, observed: 'The appellant understandably

---

[4]   See also Appeal 1981 No S24 *B D Parish*.

construes that passage as a direction not to apply for a variation of the licence for twelve months. There is no power under the Act to give such a direction . . . . Whilst it would obviously be imprudent for the appellant to make a further application until he is in a position to demonstrate to the Licensing Authority that he now exercises proper supervision over his fitters, there is no reason in law why the appellant should not make a further application for a variation within the period of twelve months from the date of the Inquiry.'

Suspension

This penalty implies suspension of the whole licence for a period determined by the Licensing Authority. 'Suspension' of a number of vehicles (ie fewer than the total authorised) from the licence, which was an order sometimes made under section 178 of the Road Traffic Act 1960, is no longer appropriate, the object being achieved by curtailment. In Appeal 1970 No G22 *James and William Kelman t/a Kelman of Turriff* the Transport Tribunal observed that 'it is provided by section 69(1) of the Transport Act 1968 that during any time of suspension the licence shall be of no effect. In other words, a suspension must be a suspension of the licence as a whole'. Suspension of the whole licence may be the appropriate order where a severe penalty, or 'short sharp shock' is called for, but where the Licensing Authority hopes and believes that the licence-holder will be able to remedy his shortcomings and reach an acceptable standard of performance within a reasonable time. Suspension may be combined with premature termination (see below) so that the Licensing Authority may satisfy himself, on a fresh application, that the operator has taken advantage of the interval to 'put his house in order'. Where the licence authorises only one vehicle, suspension of the licence rather than purported curtailment of the one vehicle is the appropriate direction.

As with revocation, suspension may have the effect of putting the operator wholly or partly out of business, and perhaps compel him to lay off his own employees and supply his transport needs by contract hire. For this reason the operator will normally seek a direction under section 69(10) for a stay of execution pending appeal (see pp 123 – 24). In Appeal 1984 No V24 *Stort Ash Company* the Deputy Licensing Authority had suspended the licence (for 15 vehicles and 8 trailers) for 2 months. The appellants successfully argued (amongst other things) that the interval of nearly 4 months between the Public Inquiry and the disposal of their appeal had given them ample time to reorganise their maintenance, and that therefore the object of the suspension order – to give them time to reorganise their business and bring the vehicles up to standard – had already been achieved. The Tribunal substituted an order for premature termination of the licence (see below).

On the other hand, in Appeal 1986 No X7 *Bradstep Limited*, also a suspension for two months, of a licence for 5 vehicles and 2 trailers, the Tribunal said: 'In our view there was ample evidence on which the Deputy Licensing Authority could conclude that the appropriate action was to suspend the licence for all the company's vehicles for two months. She adjourned for half an hour before announcing her decision and must have been fully aware of the possible serious consequences for the company.'

Section 69(7A), added to section 69 by the Road Traffic Act 1974, empowers the Licensing Authority, when he suspends a licence, to order that any vehicle specified in the licence may not be used under any other operator's licence for a period of six months, or for the remaining term of the licence, whichever is the shorter.

Premature termination

The power to order that a licence be terminated on a date earlier than that on which it would otherwise expire under section 67 of the Act was also added to section 69(1) by the Road Traffic Act 1974. It has been regularly used by the Licensing Authorities, either on its own or combined with suspension or curtailment, in order to require the licence-holder to make an earlier application for renewal, and provide evidence that warnings have been heeded and standards improved. Since the introduction on 1 June 1984 of the provisions relating to the environmental suitability of operating centres (see Chapter 3), an earlier termination of the licence and consequent application for renewal may expose the licence-holder to possible objections and/or representations on environmental grounds, but this result is incidental and is not relevant to the grounds for giving this direction. There are no decided appeals on the merits or otherwise of an order for premature termination.

Curtailment

A direction under this head removes one or more authorised vehicles from the licence either permanently or for any period which terminates before the date of expiry of the licence. It is the penalty most commonly imposed by Licensing Authorities, and may vary in effect from nominal to severe. An example of a nominal penalty is removal of vehicles from the 'margin' so that the number of vehicles specified on the licence and in actual use is not reduced. The margin can be reduced absolutely, ie so as to reduce once and for all the number of vehicles authorised by the licence, or for a period. If the Licensing Authority wishes to cut into the number of vehicles actually in use he must first remove the margin (if any), or curtail the licence by such number exceeding the margin as he wishes effectively to remove. Section 69(7A), referred to above, also empowers the Licensing Authority to order that vehicles curtailed from a licence may not be specified under any other licence for up to 6 months or the duration of the licence, whichever is the shorter period.

Unless there is a good reason for selecting particular vehicles to remove from the licence, the practice of Licensing Authorities is to leave it to the operator to select which vehicles should be removed from the licence for the period of the curtailment. If particular vehicles are nominated by the Licensing Authority they should be chosen with the objectives of the legislation in mind. Thus, in Appeal 1978 No P3 *Reginald Smith* the Tribunal observed: ' . . . the effect of choosing OFO 775R and KFO 574P had been to leave the appellant to operate his two oldest vehicles. It seems to us to be more conducive to public safety, which is the object of the legislation, that the appellant should continue to operate his newest vehicles.'

It is sometimes argued by appellants that the reduction, even temporarily, of the number of vehicles available for work will put an added burden on the remainder, and lead to lower standards of maintenance and roadworthiness; alternatively, by obliging the operator to hire in vehicles the curtailment will add a substantial and unfair financial penalty. This argument did not meet with any agreement or approval from the Tribunal in any positive sense until Appeal 1986 No X31 *R H Kitchen Ltd* was decided in February 1987. The Tribunal said: '[The appellants' counsel argued that] . . secondly the company would inevitably respond to such pressures by using its authorised vehicles more intensively than would have been the case had it been able to continue to operate 15, thereby reducing the opportunity for proper preventive maintenance . . We [also] consider that there is some force in the argument that the reduction of the appellants' fleet may have the opposite effect to that intended by the Licensing Authority.' This case was perhaps somewhat special in that the Licensing Authority had indicated that it was not his intention to affect the company's viability 'to the extent that it might not have recovered'; and the Tribunal evidently, and perhaps generously, accepted the appellants' argument that the direction would be likely to have this effect.

Conditions

Section 69(2) provides that in any case in which a direction to revoke, suspend, prematurely terminate or curtail a licence may be given, the

Licensing Authority may, alternatively or in addition, attach to the licence any, or any additional, conditions under section 66 of the Act. [5]

Warnings

A licence-holder appearing for the first time before the Licensing Authority may, unless the 'charges' are serious ones, reasonably hope to escape with a warning rather than have a more than nominal penalty imposed. In Appeal 1974 No K26 *Ernest Thorpe & Co Ltd* the Deputy Licensing Authority had remarked, with reference to the licence-holder's solicitor's plea in mitigation, that the licence-holder did not come before him merely to be let off. The Transport Tribunal observed: 'When dealing with a case in which a penalty can be imposed, the possibility that the right course may be to impose no penalty at all ought not to be excluded from consideration.' The fact that a licence-holder has already been given a warning will of course be taken into account if he has occasion to appear before the Licensing Authority a second time. Many, perhaps most, operators regard it as a penalty simply to have to appear before the Licensing Authority to answer charges relating to their operations.

Return of licences and discs

Regulation 30 of the 1984 Regulations SI No 176 deals with the administrative consequences of any order or direction affecting the number of vehicles authorised to be used under the licence. As amended by SI 1984 No 841, it requires the holder of a licence which is revoked, surrendered, suspended, prematurely terminated or curtailed to send or deliver to the Licensing Authority, on or before the date specified in a notice to that effect, the licence and the discs relating to the vehicle or vehicles affected by the order, for cancellation, retention or alteration, as the case may be. Regulation 33(1) makes failure to comply with these provisions an offence punishable by a fine as provided by section 91(6) of the Act.

---

[5] For section 66 conditions, see pp 84 – 6.

CHAPTER 9

Appeals From Licensing Authorities: Rules and Procedures

The right of appeal from decisions of Licensing Authorities to the Transport Tribunal is conferred by section 70 of the 1968 Act. The persons (including, where applicable, corporations) who may appeal are the following:

(a) applicants for the grant or variation of licences who are aggrieved by the refusal of the application or, as the case may be, by the terms or conditions of the licence or the variation, other than a limitation under section 67(3)(b);[1]

(b) licence-holders in respect of whom a direction has been given under section 61(6) for the removal of a specified vehicle from the licence; [see p 13]

(c) licence-holders in respect of whom a direction has been given under section 69(1) or 69F revoking, suspending, prematurely terminating or curtailing the licence;

(d) individuals, whether licence-holders or not, who have been disqualified from holding a licence, or from being directors of companies which hold a licence, under sections 69(5), (6) or (7);

(d) statutory objectors who, having duly made an objection to an application for a licence or the variation of a licence, are aggrieved by the grant of the application.

Alternative remedies: judicial review

Before considering in detail the procedures governing appeals to the Transport Tribunal, it will be appropriate to consider the possible

---

[1] The provision empowering the Licensing Authority to grant a licence for less than 5 years for convenience in arranging his work.

alternative remedies open to persons aggrieved by the decisions of a Licensing Authority.

The existence of a statutory right of appeal does not exclude the right of an aggrieved party to apply to the High Court for judicial review of a decision of an inferior court or tribunal, with the object of having it quashed or brought before the higher court. The remedy may be sought in cases where it is alleged that the inferior tribunal acted without jurisdiction, or exceeded its jurisdiction in some significant way. The Court will normally be slow to grant leave for judicial review where the remedy of appeal is provided by the relevant statute. It would however appear to be the only remedy directly available to persons who have unsuccessfully made representations against an application, as such persons have no right of appeal under the Act. It is true that they may now seek to be made parties to an appeal brought by an applicant or statutory objector, [2] but if no such appeal is lodged their only remedy will be through the medium of an application for judicial review, categorised as a 'costly remedy' by the Transport Tribunal in Appeal 1986 No X34 *R G & M T Jury (t/a R & G Transport)* v. *Devon County Council.*

Constitution of the Transport Tribunal

The Transport Tribunal has existed under its present name since 1947, when it was changed from the 'Railway Rates Tribunal' by the Transport Act 1947. Section 57 of the Transport Act 1962 created the Road Haulage Appeals Division of the Tribunal to hear appeals on 'carrier licensing', [3] its jurisdiction in relation to goods operator licensing being confirmed by section 94(8) and Schedule 10 of the Transport Act 1968. The constitution, powers and proceedings of the Tribunal were set out in the Tenth Schedule of the Transport Act 1962; that Schedule has now been replaced by Schedule 4 to the Transport Act 1985, in compliance with section 117(2) of that Act, which provided that Schedule 4 should have effect in place of the existing law with respect to the constitution, powers and proceedings of the Tribunal. Paragraph 9(1) of Schedule 4 declares that on an appeal from (in this context) the Licensing Authority the Tribunal shall have power:

(a)   to make such order as they think fit; or
(b)   to remit the matter to the Licensing Authority for rehearing and determination,

---

[2]   See Transport Rules 1986, Rule 14, dealt with on p 127.
[3]   Under Part IV of the Road Traffic Act 1960.

and that any such order shall be binding on the Licensing Authority. It may be assumed that 'any such order' includes an order under (b) remitting the case for rehearing. Sub-paragraph (a) sets no limits to the powers of the Tribunal on an appeal, and it is therefore open to them to make such order as seems to them the most fitting in all the circumstances. Under paragraph 14 of the Schedule an appeal can be instituted, except on questions of fact or the right to appear (*locus standi*), to the Court of Appeal in England and Wales, or the Court of Session in Scotland, in accordance with rules made by the Secretary of State.[4]

The changes in the matters covered by the successive Schedules, and in the Rules made under powers contained in those Schedules, will be examined in detail, so far as may be relevant; meanwhile the question needs to be asked, what is the effect of the successive enactment of new bodies of law on the relevance and authority of earlier appeal decisions? Appeal decisions dating from 1964 have been cited in the earlier parts of this work to illustrate, or provide authority for, certain propositions relating to the law, practice or procedure of goods operator licensing. While it is true in principle that the Transport Tribunal are not bound by their own decisions[5] and must in any case take account of changes in the substantive law of licensing, the true position must be that where the substantive law has remained essentially unchanged, appeals decided in earlier years are no less authoritative or persuasive (as the case may be) than they were originally. It is not proposed to analyse in detail the differences in constitution, powers and proceedings between those laid down in Schedule 4 to the 1985 Act and Schedule 10 to the 1962 Act. The following changes should however be mentioned as possibly affecting the operation of the Tribunal in future:

(1) the membership of the Tribunal is now as follows:

(a) a president and two or more chairman appointed by the Lord Chancellor;

(b) two or more members appointed by the Secretary of State. The President and Chairmen (known as 'judicial members') must be barristers, advocates or solicitors of 10 years' standing (for the President) and 7 years (for the Chairmen), and one of them must preside at any sitting of the Tribunal. There are no special requirements as to the qualifications or experience of the non-judicial members, who are appointed for a term in the discretion of the Secretary of State not normally extending beyond their 70th birthday;

---

[4] No rules have as yet been made.

[5] *Merchandise Transport Ltd* v. *British Transport Commission* [1962] 2 QB 173.

(2) the power to make the rules governing procedure and practice, formerly exercised by the Tribunal itself with the approval of the Lord Chancellor and the Minister of Transport, is now entrusted to the Secretary of State for Transport after consultation with the Council on Tribunals;

(3) in addition to appeals under the 1968 Act the Tribunal will hear appeals from Traffic Commissioners in relation to public service vehicles pursuant to section 50 of the Public Passenger Vehicles Act 1981; [This jurisdiction does not fall to be considered in the present context.]

(4) paragraph 9(2) of Schedule 4 to the 1985 Act provides as follows:
> '(2) The tribunal may not on any such appeal [sc. under the 1968, 1981 or 1985 Acts] take into consideration any circumstances which did not exist at the time of the determination which is the subject of the appeal.'

The significance of this provision, which is new, will be examined in its proper place (see p 133).

Rules

The Secretary of State, under paragraph 11 of the Schedule 4, may 'make general rules governing the procedure and practice of the Tribunal and generally for carrying into effect the Tribunal's duties and powers'. Paragraph 11(2) sets out six particular matters for which the rules may provide, without prejudice to the general power. These are the same as those contained in the previous Schedule 10/1962, and are as follows:

(a) the awarding of costs by the tribunal;
(b) the reference of any question to a member or officer of the tribunal, or any other person appointed by them, for report after holding a local inquiry;
(c) the review by the tribunal of decisions previously given by them;
(d) the number of members of the tribunal to constitute a quorum;
(e) enabling the tribunal to dispose of any proceedings notwithstanding that in the course of those proceedings there has been a change in the persons sitting as members of the tribunal;
(f) the right of audience before the tribunal.

In pursuance of the power in the 1962 Schedule, the tribunal duly made the Transport Tribunal Rules 1965 (SI 1965 No 1687), which were amended in 1970 and again in 1973.[6] These rules ceased to apply from the date of repeal of paragraph 11 of Schedule 10/1962, namely 15 September 1986, except in relation to appeals made before that date. The Secretary of State, under his powers in Schedule 4 to the 1985 Act, has made the Transport Tribunal Rules 1986 (SI 1986 No 1547) operative from 1 October 1986.

The 1965 and 1986 Rules compared

It is not necessary to analyse all the changes which have been made, many of which are matters of rearrangement and redrafting, but it may be useful to draw attention to the principal differences. The 1986 rules will be examined in some detail later in this chapter.

A. Old rules not reproduced

(i)   Rule 2(2) prescribed forms for most of the notices and other formal documents needed for the processing of an appeal. No forms are prescribed by the new rules.

(ii) There is now no procedure for interlocutory applications before a Registrar – rules 17 and 18.

(iii) There is no specific provision for interrogatories (rule 34), although new rule 48 (see p 133) may serve to include them.

(iv) The same comment applies to old rule 36 (Notice between parties to produce documents).

B. Innovations in new rules

(i)   Rule 14 provides for representors to apply to be made parties to an appeal. The rule-making power in Schedule 4 did not specifically include this item.

(ii) Rule 18(1) empowers the Tribunal to require the Licensing Authority 'or any party' to deliver up any documents they may require.

(iii) Rule 25(2) supplements paragraph 9(2) of Schedule 4/1985 by providing that no party may, except with the leave of the

---

6   1970 SI No 491, 1973 SI No 934.

Tribunal, cite at a hearing any evidence not given to or before the authority before the latter reached his decision.

(iv) Rule 28(4) adds to the provisions about hearings the injunction that the Tribunal 'shall so far as appears appropriate to them seek to avoid formality' in their conduct of proceedings.

(v) Rule 46 relating to the review by the Tribunal of decisions previously given by them is new, although the power to make such a rule was included in Schedule 10/1962. 'Review' is dealt with on p 133.

Procedures on appeal to the Transport Tribunal

Applications for stay of order for revocation or suspension

As already noted, section 69(10) of the 1968 Act provides that the Licensing Authority, having decided to impose a penalty under section 69, may direct that the order (for revocation, suspension etc) shall not take effect until the period for lodging an appeal to the Transport Tribunal has elapsed, and if it is lodged in time, until it has been disposed of. Most requests for a stay by those affected are granted, in order to preserve the *status quo* pending appeal, but they may be refused if the Licensing Authority considers that continued operation by the licence-holder would or might involve immediate danger to the public. In Appeal 1983 No U14 *Greatrange Ltd* the Transport Tribunal expressed the view that the Licensing Authority had treated the appellants with great leniency in allowing them to carry on operating pending the outcome of the appeal – a period of five months as it turned out. Indeed, the grant of a stay enables the operator to argue on appeal that the Licensing Authority must have considered his operation to be safe. A particular point arose in Appeal 1980 No R21 *James Sutherland (t/a Fleet Transport Services)*. The licence-holder had a licence for 6 vehicles and 8 trailers, but at the time of the Public Inquiry only 2 vehicles and 2 trailers were specified and in use. The Licensing Authority curtailed the licence to 2 vehicles and 2 trailers, and granted stay of execution pending appeal. The appellant licence-holder then proceeded to use a third vehicle from his 'margin'. The Tribunal commented: 'The normal purpose of a direction under s 69(10) is to preserve the *status quo* until the hearing of an appeal, but in this case the effect of the direction was to enable the appellant to alter the *status quo* by increasing the size of his fleet'. The Tribunal did not suggest a means by which the Licensing Authority could have preserved the appellant's right to use 2 vehicles while preventing recourse to the permitted margin. The Authority could, it is suggested, have required from the operator an undertaking that he would not take advantage of the 'margin', as the price of the grant of the stay.

If the Authority refuses to grant a stay, the licence-holder or other person concerned may apply by notice to the Tribunal for it, and the Tribunal must give their decision within 14 days. No time limit is set in the Act or Rules for the requisite notice to be lodged with the Tribunal, but it may perhaps be assumed that it must be made as soon as is reasonably practicable, and certainly before the right of appeal itself is time-barred. The Licensing Authority is sent a copy of the notice, and must supply to the Tribunal within 7 days a written statement of his reasons for refusing the stay, with a copy to the applicant. The Tribunal may at their discretion give the applicant an opportunity of being heard; if they do, the matter may be heard by one judicial member alone. The decision of the Tribunal is given in writing, with reasons, and sent to the applicant and the Authority.[7]

Procedure for appeals

Some basic advice about the procedures for appealing is contained in paragraph 56 of *A Guide to Goods Vehicle Operators Licensing* (GV74) and, in considerably more detail, in *Making an Appeal to the Transport Tribunal* (GV251A), both publications being available free from the Department of Transport. They were both published before the coming into force of the Transport Tribunal Rules 1986, SI No 1547, available from HMSO.

The 1986 Rules

The rules will be examined separately, so far as they relate to the procedures governing the way in which appeals are lodged and pursued, and the rights of appellants, respondents and other persons, eg representors.

Notice of Appeal: rules 10 and 11

Appeals are made by notice in writing served on (ie sent by post to) the Tribunal. The appellant must at the same time send copies of the notice

---

[7]   Rules 4 to 8 and 39(1) of the Transport Tribunal Rules 1986.

    (a)   to the Licensing Authority;

    (b)   if the appeal is by an applicant for a grant or variation of a licence, to every objector;

    (c)   if the appeal is by an objector, to the applicant and every other objector.

The Tribunal, by a 'proper officer', ie an officer or servant of the Tribunal so designated by the President, must send a copy of the notice to the Secretary of State. The latter requirement was not in the 1965 Rules; the Secretary of State had therefore no direct notification of the lodging of an appeal, and his attention was drawn to it (if at all) by a request from the Licensing Authority that he should become a party under (old) rule 29, in order (usually) to support the Authority's decision. There is no requirement for the Tribunal or the Licensing Authority to advise objectors of the lodging of an appeal; they must rely on being notified by the appellant under rule 10. If they are not so notified, and as a result fail to appear at the hearing, they could apply for a review under rule 46.

There is no prescribed form of notice of appeal, but rule 11(1) sets out the matters which it must contain, ie names and addresses of the appellant and the Authority, full particulars of the decision appealed from and the reasons for the appeal. Where appropriate, reasons for seeking acceptance of the appeal 'out of time' should be included. The booklet *Making an Appeal* contains a pro forma Notice of Appeal which, although no longer prescribed, is a useful guide to follow.

Time limits: rule 12

The time limit for lodging the notice of appeal is 28 days from the date of publication in *Applications and Decisions* of the decision appealed from. If, however, the decision does not appear in an issue of *Applications and Decisions* published within 21 days of the date when the decision was notified to the appellant – whether verbally at the Public Inquiry or in writing at a later time – the notice must be served on the Tribunal not later than 49 days after the latter date. In either case the count of days will exclude the date of publication or notification as the case may be. Time ceases to run when the notice is received by ('served on') the Tribunal, and not when it is put in the post. The Tribunal may however accept a notice out of time if by reason of special circumstances they think it fit and right to do so.[8]

---

[8]   For the meaning of 'special circumstances' in a different context see p 53. The Tribunal will presumably interpret the words in this context in a similarly restrictive manner.

Documents: rule 13

On receipt of his copy of the Notice of Appeal the Licensing Authority has to send to the Tribunal 6 copies of all relevant documents, including his note of the Public Inquiry, or the verbatim record if one was taken (as it nearly always is), together with a statement of the Authority's reasons for the decision appealed against. He must also supply a list of the names and addresses of representors: this requirement will be examined more fully in the context of rule 14 below. Presumably the Licensing Authority is entitled, before going to the trouble and considerable expense[9] of copying and supplying these documents, to allege that the notice was out of time (if such be the case) and to seek a ruling. Rule 13(3) requires a 'proper officer' to send to each party who requests it a copy of such of the documents received from the Authority as the party may specify. It is not clear at what stage the party specifies the documents he requires, but so far as the appellant is concerned, the request could presumably be made, in general terms, in the Notice of Appeal.

As already stated, the Tribunal expects the Authority to give reasons for his decision at or shortly after the time of making it, and not to reserve them for his response to the notice of appeal. No doubt he will take the opportunity of making his observations on the grounds of appeal, as well as elaborating as necessary on the reasons for his decision.

Notice to representors: rule 14

On receipt of an appeal in a case where representations have been made the proper officer must send to each representor a notice stating that an appeal has been made, naming the appellant, and containing a summary of the reasons for the appeal, together with a statement that the representor may within 14 days apply to the Tribunal for leave to become a party to the appeal. As has been seen, the Licensing Authority is required by rule 13 to supply the Tribunal with a list of names and addresses of representors. Both the Licensing Authority and the Tribunal may be in some difficulty in this regard: 'representor' is defined by rule 2(1) as a person who 'duly made' representations against the grant or variation of the licence in question. Many persons who write letters do not for one reason or another fulfil all the requirements of section 69B(2) as to owning or

---

[9] No order for costs can be made in favour of the Licensing Authority, whatever the outcome of the appeal. The cost of and incidental to appeals forms part of the overall cost of operator licensing, recoverable through licence fees.

occupying property in the vicinity, or the relevant rules, eg as regards being in time, sending copies to the applicant etc. The Licensing Authority will presumably have to limit his list to those representors who complied with all the requirements, or annotate the full list appropriately. A representor may well wish to challenge on appeal the Licensing Authority's decision not to accept his representation as 'duly made'.

Parties to the appeal: rules 15, 16 and 17

The parties to an appeal are:

(a) the appellant;
(b) every person to whom the appellant is required by rule 10(2)(b) or (c) to send a copy of his notice of appeal;
(c) every representor who is given leave by the Tribunal to become a party to the appeal;
(d) every person who by order of the Tribunal under rule 16 is added as a party to the appeal.

Under rule 16 the Tribunal may at any stage of an appeal order any person (other than the Authority) to be added as a party to the appeal, and give appropriate directions as to service of documents and hearing dates. Clearly it is not intended that the Licensing Authority shall ever become a party, although he may be required to produce documents to the Tribunal under rule 18 (see p 129), and he or his representative may perhaps be among those non-parties whom the Tribunal may permit to address them under rule 23(2) (see p 131). Under rule 27(1) he cannot be called as a witness, although presumably a member of his staff could be.

It is possible that rule 16(1) would enable the Tribunal to have the Secretary of State added as a party to the appeal in cases where he had exercised his right to appear and be heard under paragraph 12(2) of Schedule 4 of the Transport Act 1985. The various rules relating to parties, ie rule 24, 25 and 26, would then apply to the Secretary of State in his capacity as a party. He is in any case under a duty, under the same paragraph, to give the Tribunal such assistance as they may reasonably require. It may be mentioned at this point that the Tribunal occasionally invite the Treasury Solicitor to instruct Counsel as a friend of the court *(amicus curiae)* to assist the Tribunal on points of law. Counsel will not, as such, represent the Secretary of State or any other party.[10]

---

[10] See, for example, Appeals 1986 X17 *Sunnyside Removals* and X25 *Hay and Straw Services.* In both cases Counsel for the Treasury Solicitor submitted arguments contrary to the Licensing Authority's interpretation of the law. The Licensing Authority had no opportunity to reply to these arguments.

Rule 17 provides for what in the 1965 Rules were referred to as 'pleadings', namely written replies of parties to the reasons for the appeal, and any further written statements which the Tribunal may require to be supplied. Time limits are prescribed for replies and other statements. Rule 25 lays down that parties may not, unless the Tribunal think it just to allow them to do so, put forward or rely on grounds to support or oppose an appeal which they have not stated in their notice of appeal or written reply as the case may be.

Discovery of documents: rule 18

In Appeal 1979 No Q17 *D R & M L Winsor (t/a Valley Services)* the Tribunal decided that they had no power to order the Licensing Authority to produce documents under the 1965 rules, as rule 37 limited the power to requiring production by 'any party'. New rule 18 provides that the Tribunal 'shall' require the Authority or any party to deliver to the Tribunal any document in their possession or power which the Tribunal may wish to see. This is therefore a new provision supplying what was perhaps considered to be a deficiency in the light of the *Valley Services* case. The document for which the appellants in that case sought an order to produce was the brief prepared for the Licensing Authority by his staff for use at the Public Inquiry. The Tribunal decided that, even if the brief was among the documents which rule 14A (now rule 13) required the Licensing Authority to send to the Tribunal, they had no power under the Act or rules to order the Authority to produce it. They did not indicate whether they would have made an order if they had had the power. It remains to be seen whether the Tribunal will order production of briefs and other reports which form part of the material which the Authority or his advisors routinely consider before calling an operator to account.

Rule 18(2) provides that the power to require production may not be exercised in relation to any document which the Authority or party could not be compelled to produce in an action in the courts in England or Scotland as the case might be. The grounds for resisting production would be that it was against the public interest for the document to be produced, or that it was privileged by reason of confidentiality or otherwise. If the Authority or other party by whom a document is required to be produced asserts that the document is privileged, the issue will presumably have to be tried by the Tribunal; and their decision, if adverse to the Authority or party concerned, would be open to appeal to the Court of Appeal, or Court of Session in Scotland, under paragraph 14 of Schedule 4.

Preliminary points of law: rule 19

Rule 19 provides as follows:

> '19. (1) The Tribunal may order any point of law which appears to be in issue in the appeal to be determined at a preliminary hearing.
>
> (2) If, in the opinion of the Tribunal, the determination of that point substantially disposes of the whole appeal, the Tribunal may treat the preliminary hearing as the hearing of the appeal and may make such order by way of disposing of the appeal as the Tribunal think fit.
>
> (3) If the parties so agree in writing the Tribunal may determine the point without a hearing, but in any such cases and without prejudice to rule 29(3), the Tribunal may not at the same time dispose of the appeal.'

With the addition of sub-rule (3), which is new, this reproduces old rule 20, with the perhaps essential difference that under the latter rule the Tribunal could set a case down for preliminary hearing only on the application of one or more of the parties. There is no record in the judgments given in appeals since 1961 that a preliminary hearing on a point of law was held in any of those cases. As the rule now stands the Tribunal may either respond to an application by a party or order the preliminary hearing on its own initiative. It seems, indeed, that the Tribunal may order a preliminary hearing of their own motion on a point of law not raised in the notice of appeal or replies to it. However, if the preliminary hearing has been ordered on the application of a party, that party may not put forward at the hearing any grounds not stated in the application. rule 25(1).

Whether the preliminary hearing disposes of the whole appeal may in some case be foreseeable, but in others will not become clear until the preliminary hearing is concluded. An example of a point of law which might be the subject of such a hearing is the question whether objectors and representors are entitled to appear or be represented at the hearing of an applicant's 'special representations' under section 69C(5).[11] An issue which might conceivably have been determined without a hearing under rule 19(3) is the meaning of 'parking' under section 69B(3), ie whether it means both active movement and static conditions.[12] Rule 29(3), referred to in rule 19(3), provides generally that the Tribunal may determine any appeal without a hearing if all the parties so agree in writing. The expression 'without prejudice to

[11] See discussion of Appeal 1986 No X10 *West Lancashire District Council* v. *Ken Abram Ltd* on p 73.
[12] See p 75 re Appeal 1985 No W23 *D & A Transport and Others* v. *Lancashire County Council and Others.*

rule 29(3)' presumably enables the parties to agree that the preliminary determination of a point of law without hearing should dispose of the appeal.

Hearings: rules 20 to 25

These rules lay down the procedure for giving notice of hearings, attendance of parties and witnesses, conduct of hearings, etc. It will be sufficient to draw attention to a limited number of salient points.

Hearings in public: rule 22 The public have access to hearings unless the Tribunal consider there are exceptional reasons for holding a hearing in private. Even at a hearing which is in essence public, the Tribunal may exclude such members of the public as they think fit from that part of a hearing where the 'appropriate financial standing' of any person is to be considered. Since under rule 23(1) all the parties may appear at any hearing in connection with an appeal, it seems clear that 'members of the public' under rule 22 are those persons attending as spectators who are neither parties, representatives of parties nor bona fide witnesses. Apart from the particular power under rule 22(4) to exclude any person whose conduct has disrupted or is likely to disrupt the progress of the hearing, parties of whatever kind, ie including representors given leave under rule 15(c), have the right to be present throughout.[13]

Appearance at hearings: rule 23 As stated above, all parties have a right to appear. Rule 23(2) enables the Tribunal to permit anyone at all 'whom they deem likely to be able to assist' to address them on specified points of law or fact. This provision was in the old rules (rule 28), but there is nothing in the appeal judgments to indicate that the power has ever been used. The provision is perhaps wide enough to include the Licensing Authority whose decision is under appeal, but more likely persons would perhaps be experts, eg on noise abatement, or planning law or practice.

Rule 25, which limits the grounds of appeal or objection to those 'pleaded', has already been referred to.[14] Rule 25(2) further precludes a party from citing evidence before the Tribunal which was not given to or before the authority prior to his reaching the decision appealed against. So far as this rule is concerned, the Tribunal have a discretion under rule 25(4) to allow grounds not pleaded to be put forward, and evidence to be cited which was not before the Licensing Authority. The legal effect of this provision may however be open to doubt in the light of paragraph 9(2) of Schedule 4 to the Transport Act 1985, cited above. The rules cannot override the statutory provision.

---

[13] Of the discussion on the rights of appearance at public inquiries on pp 57 – 66.
[14] See under rule 17 on p 128 and under rule 19 on p 130.

Rules 26, 27, 28 and 29 deal with evidence by affidavit, attendance of witnesses. conduct of proceedings, consolidation of appeals and adjournments. Rule 27 gives the Tribunal, on the application of any party, power to summon any person other than the Authority 'to attend any hearing as a witness'. The wording of 'old' rule 33 on the same subject allowed the summons to require the witness to produce documents, and a schedule prescribed separate forms, Form 9 relating to the giving of oral evidence, and Form 10 to the production of documents. The 1986 rules neither includes the summoning of a witness to produce documents, nor prescribes any form of witness summons. The expression 'to attend any hearing as a witness' is perhaps wide enough to cover production of documents; rule 48, referred to below, may in any event supply any want of a specific rule in this regard. Rule 29(3), allowing determination of an appeal without a hearing if all parties agree in writing, has already been mentioned (see discussion of rule 19 on p 129).

Rule 30 sets out the rules for announcing, recording and distributing the decision of the Tribunal. All findings of fact, and a statement of the reasons for the decision, must be set out in a document to be signed and dated by the president or another judicial member.

Review of decisions: rule 46
This is a new provision which did not appear in the 1965 rules. Rule 46(1) and (2) provide as follows:

'46 (1) The Tribunal may review, and revoke or vary by certificate signed by the president, any decision if a party applies to them for the purpose and satisfies them that
(a) being a party who was entitled to be heard at a hearing but who failed to appear at that hearing he had a good and sufficient reason for failing to appear;
(b) in any case, the interests of justice require such a review.
(2) An application for the purposes of paragraph (1) of this rule shall be made in writing
(a) if it relates to an application to which Part II of these rules applies,[15] within 14 days of the date when the decision in question was made, and
(b) in any other case, within 28 days of that date,
and shall contain a full statement of the grounds for the application.'

The right to apply for a review is limited to parties, and therefore excludes the Licensing Authority, but could perhaps include the

---

[15] Ie appeals from a refusal of a 'stay' – see p 124.

Secretary of State, if he has been made a party under rule 16(1) (see p 128). An application may be summarily refused by the president if in his opinion it has no reasonable prospect of success. If it is accepted, the Tribunal will proceed to a review of the decision, which will take the form of a re-hearing in accordance with the provisions of the rules applicable to appeals. The onus, on an applicant for review, of satisfying the Tribunal under rule 46(1)(a) that he or she had a good and sufficient reason for failing to appear at the original appeal hearing, is likely to be a heavy one, especially if no serious attempt had been made to obtain an adjournment of the hearing in the first place.[16]

The ground for review under rule 46(1)(b), namely that the interests of justice require it, is so wide as to be incapable of definition or categorisation.[17] It is relevant to note – in order to exclude a possible ground for a review application – that paragraph 9(2) of Schedule 4 to the Transport Act 1985 forbids the Tribunal, on appeal from a Licensing Authority, to take into consideration any circumstances which did not exist at the date of the Authority's decision. Moreover, an appeal on a point of law can be instituted separately from the Tribunal to the Court of Appeal (or Court of Session in Scotland). The Tribunal are unlikely to grant an application for review on the grounds that their decision on the facts or merits was wrong, at least if all the evidence was before them; especially as by rule 46(4)(a) the Tribunal hearing the review must so far as possible consist of the same members as heard the appeal. However, a possible ground for review of the decision might be that its correctness was put in doubt by a subsequent decision of a higher court on a similar case, or possibly a planning decision by the Secretary of State for the Environment.

Superior court practice: rule 48

This rule provides that where not inconsistent with the rules, the general principles of practice, or any particular practice, of the superior court may be adopted and applied as the Tribunal may think fit. 'Superior court' is defined by rule 2(1) as meaning, in England and Wales, the Supreme Court of Judicature, and in Scotland the Court of Session. This rule reproduces, with an insignificant change of wording, rule 47 of the 1965 rules, and no new principle is involved. The provision is so general, and the scope given by it to the Tribunal so wide, that it could perhaps be used to supply any

---

[16] An objector may perhaps not have been served with the Notice of Appeal; see p 125 above.

[17] There are however precedents in the Industrial Tribunals (Rules of Procedure) SI 1985 No 16, and the Date Protection Tribunal Rules SI 1985 No 1568.

particular deficiency in the rules, eg as regards the summoning of witnesses (see p 132), interrogatories and discovery of documents between parties (see p 129). The only example in the reported appeal judgments of the principle of the rule (ie 'old' rule 47) being applied is the reference to Court of Appeal Practice regarding 'fresh evidence' in Appeal 1986 No X31 *R H Kitchen Ltd*, dealt with on p 137 below.

Costs: rule 49

Rule 43(3) of the 1965 rules stated that the costs of and incidental to any proceedings should be in the discretion of the court (ie the Tribunal), provided that no order for costs should be made unless in the opinion of the court the proceedings or any objection or representation were frivolous or vexatious. Rule 49 of the 1986 Rules makes two significant changes, namely:

> (i) any order for costs must be 'against one party and in favour of such other party or parties as may be specified. . .'.

It is clear that – whatever the position under the previous rules – no order for costs can in any event be made for or against the Licensing Authority, although the Secretary of State, if made a party, could, it would appear, be the subject of an order;

> (ii) under rule 49(2) an order against a party may only be made if the Tribunal consider that the party in question 'has been responsible for frivolous, vexatious, improper or unreasonable action in making, pursuing or resisting an appeal . .'.

The addition of 'improper' and 'unreasonable' to 'frivolous' and 'vexatious' widens the discretion of the Tribunal substantially, and will enable them, for instance, to visit with costs a party bringing an unmeritorious appeal. Indeed, in Appeal 1986 No X34 *R G and M T Jury (t/a R & G Transport)* v. *Devon County Council* an order for costs was made in favour of representors who had been made parties, the Tribunal holding that the appeal never had a reasonable prospect of success.[18] It may perhaps be expected that an appellant whose case is that he has 'put his house in order' subsequently to the Authority's determination runs the risk of being visited with costs on the ground that his action in making the appeal was unreasonable, since evidence of matters occurring since the determination cannot be

---

[18] See p 74–5 for comment on this Appeal. No order for costs was made against the appellant Council in Appeal 1987 No Y2 *Daventry District Council* v. *Wrights Road Haulage,*, although the submission which was the basis of the appeal was 'doomed from the start'.

taken into account.[19] However, a party 'resisting an appeal' would by definition have a decision wholly or partly in his favour, and his action would, it is suggested, rarely be held to be improper or unreasonable.

The question of costs in any particular case is wholly open to argument, in the light of the alterations in the rules, and very little if any assistance can be got from past appeal decisions. An order for costs may be for a specific sum, or for costs to be taxed on one of the scales prescribed for civil proceedings in the county court in England.[20] or the sheriff court in Scotland. It seems that the taxation would be carried out by the county court or the sheriff court, as the case might be, and not by an officer of the Tribunal, as was provided by rule 43(2) of the 1965 rules. Any order of the Tribunal may be enforced by execution, in England and Wales, as if it were an order of the High Court, and in Scotland may be recorded for execution in the books of council and session and be enforceable accordingly.[21]

---

[19] By reason of paragraph 9(2) of Scheulde 4 to the Transport Act 1985, the text which is set out on p 122 above.

[20] In the *Jury* appeal the order was for taxation on County Court scale 3.

[21] Paragraph 8(3) of Schedule 4 to the Transport Act 1985.

CHAPTER 10

The Hearing of Appeals: Principles and Procedures

The nature of the appeal process

In essence an appeal to the Transport Tribunal against a decision by a Licensing Authority is not a re-hearing of the case, with evidence being given over again by the parties and their witnesses. As has been seen, the rules make provision, exceptionally, for non-parties to address the Tribunal (rule 23(2) see p 127), or for parties to give evidence and call witnesses (rule 18(2)). In the great majority of appeals, however, the Tribunal hear argument based on the record of the Public Inquiry and the reasoned decision and further observations, if any, of the Licensing Authority, the appellant being concerned – personally or by representative – to persuade the Tribunal that the decision was wholly or partly erroneous.

Rule 28(4) gives the Tribunal a discretion, subject to the rules, to conduct the proceedings at any hearing in such matter as they may determine, and directs them to seek to avoid formality. Rule 45 provides that proceedings shall not be rendered void by reason only of an irregularity from failure – presumably on anyone's part – to comply with any provision of the rules before the Tribunal have reached their decision; in such a case the Tribunal are to take such steps to cure the irregularity as they think fit.

Further evidence on appeal.

Rule 30(2) of the 1965 rules allowed the Tribunal to hear new evidence if they thought it just to do so. In exercising their discretion under that rule the Tribunal generally applied two principles:

(i) In relation to evidence of matters existing at the date of the hearing before the Licensing Authority, they allowed it to be given if it was clearly relevant and there was some adequate reason for its not having been put before the Authority. Thus in Appeal 1966 No C73 *C Rudman & Sons Ltd* the Tribunal allowed evidence to be given corroborating certain statements which the Licensing Authority had not believed. They said: 'Having regard to the way in which the Licensing Authority expressed his decision, it seemed to us that this was material which might possibly have affected his decision had it been before him, and furthermore it was material the absence of which at the inquiry could not be ascribed to lack of due diligence on the part of the appellants and their advisers. We accordingly decided to admit this evidence'. On the other hand, in Appeal 1976 No N1 *Dennis Clemetson* (one example among many), the appellant sought to put before the Tribunal certain exculpatory statements which he did not give to the Licensing Authority, having in fact left the inquiry before the hearing was completed. The Tribunal said: 'We cannot too strongly emphasise that it is not the function of this Court to consider material which could have been but was not put before the Licensing Authority . . . '

(ii) In relation to matters arising since the decision appealed from – eg fresh arrangements made for maintenance, new premises occupied etc – the Tribunal usually declined to substitute themselves for the Licensing Authority as a court of first instance, and would either dismiss the appeal, with or without a postponement of the effective date of the order to enable a fresh application to be made, without damage meanwhile to the operator's business,[1] or remit the case for further hearing by the Licensing Authority. The latter course would be adopted in particular in cases which the Tribunal thought that the new material would be likely to impress the Licensing Authority favourably, and that the operator should not be put out of business meanwhile.

There is no reason to suppose that the approach of the Tribunal to cases in the first category – evidence of matters existing at the time of the decision – will be any different in the future. However, as regards category (ii), paragraph 9(2) of Schedule 4 to the Transport Act 1985 has enacted that the Tribunal may not take into consideration any circumstances which did not exist at the time of the Authority's determination. Rule 25(2) also states: ' . . . a party shall not be entitled to adduce any evidence not given to or before the authority prior to the authority reaching the decision appealed against.' These statutory provisions would seem to prevent the Tribunal from admitting evidence or argument about matters subsequent to the decision appealed from, or at any rate from taking it into consideration in deciding whether to allow the appeal or remit the case for hearing under paragraph 9(1) of Schedule 4. There are provisions in the rules – eg rule 26 (evidence by affidavit), rule 27

---

[1]   As, for instance, in Appeal 1974 No L12 *M J Hope*.

(attendance of witnesses), and rule 28(2) (party may give evidence and call witnesses) – which allow such evidence to be given to the Tribunal; but it must be assumed that such evidence cannot relate to 'circumstances which did not exist at the time of the determination'. The provisions of Schedule 4, being part of an Act of Parliament, must prevail over anything in the rules.

Appeal 1986 No X31 *R H Kitchen Ltd* has to be examined in the light of these provisions. The date of the Public Inquiry at which the decision appealed from was made (28 October 1986) indicates that the relevant provision of Schedule 4 was effective and in force when the appeal was lodged. The Licensing Authority had given a direction curtailing the licence on the basis, clearly implied in his decision, that this would not seriously affect the viability of the operator's business. The appellants sought to put before the Tribunal forecasts of profit and loss for the year ending 31 December 1987, prepared by accountants subsequently to the decision. These forecasts, if accepted, would show that the business would in fact be prejudiced. The Tribunal admitted this evidence in reliance (partly at least) on Court of Appeal practice:[2] 'In this context we bear in mind that the Court of Appeal will admit fresh evidence *inter alia* as to matters happening since the date of the trial which substantially affects (sic) a basic assumption made at the trial.' The Tribunal do not seem to have regarded as relevant – far less as overriding – the provision of paragraph 9(2) of Schedule 4 referred to above, as no reference is made to it in the judgment. They may perhaps have treated the financial forecasts drafted after the inquiry as merely putting on paper evidence which already existed at the date of the inquiry – although this would seem to make the Court of Appeal authority about *fresh* evidence strictly irrelevant.

The Tribunal's judgment in this appeal also appears to give support to the argument not infrequently put forward on appeals from orders for curtailment of licences, to the effect that the reduction of the number of vehicles available to do the work will put an added burden on the remainder, with consequent deterioration in standards of maintenance.[3]

The Transport Tribunal is, and always has been, a court of record: see now Transport Act 1985, Schedule 4 paragraph 1. (The categorisation is of no practical significance in the context of this book.[4]) It is not, however, bound by its own decisions, at any rate where no principle of law is involved, but discretion has to be

---

[2]   See commentary on rule 48, p 133.
[3]   See p 117 for comment on this decision in relation to curtailment.
[4]   For the meaning of 'court of record' see Halsbury, *Laws of England* (4th Edition) Vol 10 paragraph 709.

exercised on the merits of a case. The Tribunal in such cases feel themselves free to depart from what might appear to be a precedent. An example of this type of case is Appeal 1981 No S11 *William North Curtis*: the Licensing Authority had revoked the licence, and the appellant argued that although he could apply for a fresh licence, to allow the revocation to stand meanwhile would impose a penalty of indefinite duration. The Tribunal said: 'In support of this argument Mr Hird cited the decisions of this Court in *Joseph Goldsmith Lucas* (1979) No Q14 and *B H Transport* (1980) No R9, in each of which we gave a decision which would have the effect of keeping the appellant on the road until any application for a new licence had been determined. In giving these decisions we were not purporting to lay down a general rule applicable in all cases. Indeed it would have been wrong for us to do so, for we are not bound by our own decisions: see *Merchandise Transport Ltd* v. *British Transport Commission* (1962) 2 QB 173.'

This is not to say, however, that considered decisions, following argument, on essential issues of law arising from the interpretation of the Acts and Regulations, would not be followed, as was exemplified by the series of cases following and applying *Cash and McCall*. This would be so even if there was some initial uncertainty, eg as to whether section 69B(5) relating to 'material change' applies to variation applications.[5] The view expressed, and acted on, in the case which is the current authority on this point,[6] is unlikely to be changed unless and until the Court of Appeal (or Court of Session in Scotland) rules otherwise on an appeal under paragraph 14 of Schedule 4, or the Act is amended.

Matters of fact and judgment

The peculiar position of the Licensing Authority in the exercise of his functions was illustrated in Appeal 1966 No C12 *Transport Holding Company*. The customary use of the expression 'quasi-judicial' to describe his position reflects the fact that he is primarily exercising the administrative function of issuing licences; he is also monitoring performance and initiating enforcement action. He has a day-to-day working knowledge of the operators in his area – especially perhaps of those on whom he has received adverse reports. He has detailed knowledge of conditions in his Area, and has visited operators'

---

[5] Appeals 1985 Nos W8 *R G Bown t/a RGB Transport* and W23 *D & A Transport Ltd and Others* v. *Lancashire County Council and Another*.
[6] Appeal 1986 No X10 *Ken Abram Ltd* v. *West Lancashire District Council*.

premises and attended road checks etc to a greater or lesser extent. He is entitled, in reaching decisions on matters coming before him, to make use of his own local knowledge, subject to the operator concerned being informed as to what his information is in the particular case, and having an opportunity to challenge or contest it, or give evidence relating to it.

One particular aspect of the Licensing Authority's partly administrative, partly judicial function, is that he is entitled to look 'behind the curtain' of incorporation where limited liability companies are concerned, and take into account the actions of individuals who – whatever their formal position in the company – are in effective control of its operations. The authority for this proposition is the Court of Appeal decision in *Merchandise Transport Ltd* v. *British Transport Commission and Others* (1962) 2 QB 173. While all the judgments given in the case are illuminating, it is sufficient for present purposes to cite one sentence from the judgment of Lord Justice (as he then was) Sellers: 'In an administrative matter of this kind where licences have to be obtained and granted for the efficient provision and regulation of road transport and where discretion has to be exercised on the information available, I think the authority is justified in looking at the substance of the matter and where effective control lies . . '

It is a generally accepted principle, where appeals are not dealt with by way of re-hearing, that the appeal court does not interfere with the lower court's findings of fact, unless there was no evidence on which such findings could have been reached, or they are otherwise against the weight of evidence. Equally, the appeal court will not normally substitute its own view of the facts for that of the court below, so long as the conclusion reached by that court – in this context the Licensing Authority – was not one that no reasonable Licensing Authority could have reached. It is of course important that the Licensing Authority should clearly set out his findings of fact and the conclusions he draws from them.[7]

It is perhaps especially important that the Licensing Authority's findings of fact and conclusions should be clearly stated in cases where environmental factors are in issue. For instance, whether a given amount of noise or other source of environmental complaint attributable to the use of an operating centre as such is sufficient to effect prejudicially the use or enjoyment of certain property is primarily a matter for the subjective judgment of the property owner, unless indeed there is evidence, for example, of actual noise

---

[7] Appeal 1985 No W23 *D & A Transport Ltd & Others* v. *Lancashire County Council & Another*.

levels as compared with what is generally accepted as tolerable in a given environment. Moreover the effect on the owner or occupier of property has to be weighed against such other factors as the general character of the neighbourhood, the background to the operation, the method of conducting it, the existence of other sources of environmental complaint, etc. The Tribunal have stated (see p 77) that they would be slow to interfere with the conclusions reached by the Licensing Authority after due and careful consideration of all the evidence and argument, provided that there was no error of law.

Their task in this respect is not made easier by the fact that in many appeals, especially those from decisions under section 69, they hear argument from one side only. The Licensing Authority is never a party to appeals brought under the Act and rules (see p 128). In appeals other than those arising from decisions under the environmental provisions of sections 69A to 69G – in which there is always likely to be an actual or potential respondent[8] – nearly all appeal hearings involve only the one party. There is no one present at the hearing to respond to or challenge the appellant's statements, for instance, as to what a particular passage in the record means; or to object to the appellant's putting doubtfully justified glosses on the recorded evidence, or even inserting new evidence in the guise of such glosses.

The Tribunal are of course fully alive to the limitations inherent in appeals involving one side only, and make appropriate allowances. In Appeal 1975 No M3 *Henry James Garner t/a Prim Removals* they appreciated that the case was put to them by counsel on appeal differently from the way it was put to the Licensing Authority. They said: ' . . if the appellant's case had been presented to the Licensing Authority in the way it has been presented to us, it seems more likely that the Licensing Authority would have taken a different view of the matter. In saying that, of course, I am not unmindful of the fact that we have only heard one side of the case today, but that is a difficulty which is inherent in practically all appeals relating to operators' licences, since the appeals in which there are, or indeed can be, respondents, are very few indeed.'

The position described in this passage was changed by the implementation of Schedule 4 to the Transport Act 1982, allowing objections and representations on environmental grounds. Thus since 1 June 1984 a substantial proportion of appeals have included both parties; it is possible, indeed, that the involvement of local councils in appeals arising under sections 69A to 69G has alerted

---

[8] Because applications cannot be refused on environmental grounds unless objections and/or representations have been lodged.

them to the possibility of objecting to applications under section 63, on such grounds as 'fit person', good repute, financial standing, etc.

As already stated, only 'statutory objectors' have a right of appeal; representors may now apply to be made parties to an appeal already lodged, [9] which will have been done either by an applicant or a statutory objector. Their not having a right of appeal is not however a reason for the Licensing Authority to tilt the balance in their favour at the initial hearing of the case. In Appeal 1985 No W4 *R A Nightingale t/a Anglia Fruiterers* the Tribunal said: 'A Licensing Authority will frequently have to balance the interests of an applicant for a licence against the interests of representors whose enjoyment of their land will to some extent be adversely affected by the grant of the licence. In balancing those conflicting interests a Licensing Authority must not, in our judgment, make an order more favourable to a representor than he would have made if Parliament had granted representors a right of appeal.'

On the other hand, the lack of any right of appeal by representors enhances the need for their representations to be carefully considered before they are rejected for some failure to comply with regulations, perhaps by the staff of the Licensing Authority in accordance with routine instructions. In Appeal 1986 No X34 *R G & M T Jury (t/a R & G Transport)* v. *Devon County Council* the Tribunal expressed the view that 'sieving' of representations by staff before being brought to the attention of the Licensing Authority himself required careful consideration and control (see p 54).

---

[9]   Under rule 14, see p 127.

CHAPTER 11

Developments in the Legislation

Like most public Acts devised for the purpose of controlling the activities of industrial operators in the general and special interests of the public – including the industry itself – the Transport Act 1968 has been the subject of scrutiny from time to time to determine whether improvements are required to give better effect to its intentions, or indeed to amend or extend its scope. There have been two major inquiries into the workings of the Act: namely the Foster Committee's inquiry and report in 1977 – 8, referred to on p 10 of this book, and the inquiry and report of Sir Arthur Armitage published in December 1980 under the title *Lorries, People and the Environment*. This was not primarily, or even substantially, an inquiry into operator licensing as such, but the role of Licensing Authorities in controlling the effect of heavy lorries on people and the environment was dealt with in Chapter 6 under the general heading of 'Getting lorries away from people'.

The working of operator licensing was also made the subject of scrutiny by Lord Rayner as part of an examination of governmental policies and procedures, with the primary object of improving efficiency, elimating waste and 'bureaucratic' practices, and consequently reducing the cost of administering the system. Some of the recommendations proposed by Rayner – eg that operators' licences should be continuous until terminated by revocation or surrender – have been the subject of public consultation with the industry and other interested parties. Other topics such as improvement of enforcement practices, drivers' licensing and conduct of road checks, are not within the scope of this book. It will however be relevant to consider some of the suggestions in the various reports relating to the provisions concerning 'environmental' issues.

The Foster Committee stated at the outset of the first chapter of their Report that in their judgment the purpose of operator licensing should be to promote road safety, to help protect the environment from heavy goods vehicles, and to prevent undue damage to the roads. Their recommendations as regards the first and last of these objectives were directed to such matters as the tightening up and enforcement of drivers' licensing, drivers' hours and weight limits, and organisation of Traffic Area work (mention of which was made on p10). They also made a number of recommendations on the environmental issue, to which indeed they devoted a chapter (Chapter 9) of the Report. Their major recommendations on this topic were as follows:

'(25) that the statutory definition of an operating centre should be revised to give effect to the original intention of controlling its environmental impact;[2]

(26) that a Licensing Authority should not renew the licence of an operator whose operating centre is in breach of development control where the local planning authority is already taking enforcement action;

(27) that, except where planning permission has been expressly granted for the use of the operating centre, a Licensing Authority should not grant a licence unless he is satisfied that the centre is environmentally suitable;

(28) that a Licensing Authority should be able to impose conditions on a licence to deal with environmental matters;

(29) that a Licensing Authority should have a duty, when considering environmental issues, to take into account the views of the appropriate local planning and highway authorities, other statutory objectors, any residents or non-residential occupiers of property in the proximity of the operating centre, and indeed any person offended by the activities of vehicles from that operating centre.'[1]

Of these five recommendations, nos (25), (28) and most of (29) were endorsed by Armitage, and became the starting point for that part of the Transport Act 1982, ie section 52 and Schedule 4, which added the environmental suitability of the operating centre as a major consideration in the granting of licences, and extended rights of objection beyond the 'statutory objectors'. It may be noted that recommendation (27), which puts the onus on an applicant to prove environmental suitability in the absence of express planning

---

[1]   ie in the amendment to s.64(2)(d) discussed on p 23.

permission, was not taken up by Armitage and did not become part of the law. Also, the final 14 words of recommendation (29) were, it seems, regarded as casting the net of possible 'representors' altogether too wide.

Armitage did not endorse recommendation (26), which the Foster Committee said (para 9.16) 'would avoid the absurdity of one government agency permitting what another is lawfully seeking to prevent'. As has been seen, the Transport Tribunal in the 1982 appeal of *Cameron Shuttering* did not consider this to be an absurdity, and have since repeated their view that the two matters are entirely separate, and that the Licensing Authority does not exercise their functions to assist the Planning Authority (see p 80). Armitage, for his part, recognised (para 272) the danger of turning hearings of applications for licences into substitute planning inquiries, and recommended that any additional powers for Licensing Authorities should be as specific as possible. His final recommendations relating to operator licensing were as follows:

' 23. In the licensing of operators, the definition of "operating centre" should be extended so that it includes lorry depots and other places where the operator customarily parks his lorries when they are not away on business.

24. Licensing Authorities should be empowered to take into account environmental factors in deciding whether operating centres are suitable and to impose specific conditions on licences relating to where and when lorries should park, and their number, size and type.

25. The Licensing Authority should be empowered to reject an application on the grounds that intensification of the use of a operating centre would make it unsuitable on environmental grounds.

26. The statutory duty of the Licensing Authorities should be widened to include a duty to take account of views which local authorities submit to them on applications for licences.'

The Armitage Report did not deal in terms with the right of residents to object or make representations about licence applications on environmental grounds. The final form of the relevant provisions of the 1982 Act represented a selection of the principal recommendations of the two Reports, as modified in the light of representations from the various interests affected or likely to be affected by the legislation.

The industry were successful, during the preparation of the Bill which became the Transport Act 1982, in persuading the drafters to include the provision, now section 69B(5), precluding refusal of an application if the grant of it would involve no 'material change', and the connected provision that stringent conditions whose operation could in effect nullify the grant should not be imposed without giving the applicant a special hearing.[2] The industry, it is fair to say, regard this outcome as satisfactory as far as it goes. They would like the principle of 'existing use rights' to be extended so that (i) renewal applications where there is no material change need not be advertised, and (ii) persons or companies taking over existing operating centres on a 'walk-in walk-out' basis can dispense with application, or at least with advertisement. It has already been noted that this is what happens in effect when a company changes hands by the transfer of its shares.

The other principal point being made at that time was that a business using heavy goods vehicles might identify an apparently suitable site, obtain outline planning permission, arrange finance, have building plans prepared and so on, and then find that their application for an operator's licence involving use of that place is objected to, and perhaps refused or granted with onerous conditions. The argument was advanced that a procedure analogous to outline planning permission was required to enable a site to be passed as a suitable operating centre at an early stage. The situation here envisaged has not manifested itself in any of the appeals so far decided, but the issue is still live.

From the opposite side of the debate, it has been represented that the rights of the public and interested bodies to be heard should be augmented in one or more of the following ways:

(a) Parish Councils should be given the right to object or make representations on their own behalf;

(b) environmental interest groups should have the right to make representations in their own name, and not only through the medium of individual representors who are 'qualified';

(c) persons who duly made representations and appeared at the public inquiry should have a right of appeal;

(d) the right of people to complain about environmental nuisance from operating centres should be enlarged:

(i) by including the operations of and relating to vehicles having business there ('visiting vehicles') and not only the vehicles authorised under the licence;

(ii) by extending the distance from the operating centre within which residents may claim to be affected in the use or enjoyment of their property.

---

[2] For discussion of material change, see pp 69 – 72.

In 1986 the Department of Transport carried out an internal review of the environmental provisions introduced by the 1982 Act, and announced a list of amendments which would be proposed as soon as opportunity arose. These would have the following objectives:

(a) to make it clear that the environmental effects, within the vicinity of an operating centre, of authorised vehicles moving to or from the centre are a relevant consideration;

(b) to limit the use of operating centres by operators with centres in more than traffic area;

(c) to extend the range of activities involving authorised vehicles at an operating centre subject to control;

(d) to consider ways of providing for itinerant operators;

(e) to allow Parish Councils to make environmental representations;

(f) to reduce the need to advertise applications in all cases;

(g) to provide that an interim licence does not give existing use status.

It will be noted that item (g) has already been achieved through a Transport Tribunal decision[3], and it is not impossible that some others in the list might be dealt with in the same way – see for instance the discussion of Appeal 1985 No W17 *Surrey Heath Borough Council* v. *NFT Distribution Ltd* on pp 49 – 50, as relating to items (a) and (c). The list does not include any proposal for extending the subjects of complaint to include visiting vehicles, or giving representors a right of appeal. In any case, there has been no indication of when an opportunity might arise to introduce the necessary legislation.

---

[3] Appeal 1986 No X29 *Kirk Brothers Ltd* v. *Macclesfield District Council:* see pp 69 – 70.

Vehicles for Which an Operator's Licence is Not Required

Schedule 5 to the Goods Vehicles (Operators' Licences, Qualifications and Fees) Regulations 1984 SI 1984 No 176 as amended by the Goods Vehicles (Operators' Licences, Qualifications and Fees)(Amendment) Regulations 1986 SI 1986 No 666;
and by the Goods Vehicles (Operators' Licences, Qualifications and Fees)(Amendment) Regulations 1987 SI 1987 No 841

1. Any vehicle (including a trailer drawn by it) mentioned in paragraph 2(1) of Part I of Schedule 3 to the Vehicles (Excise) Act 1971 whilst being used solely for the haulage of such objects as are referred to in that paragraph.

2. A dual-purpose vehicle and any trailer drawn by it.

3. A vehicle used on a road only in passing from private premises to other private premises in the immediate neighbourhood belonging (except in the case of a vehicle so used only in connection with excavation or demolition) to the same person, provided that the distance travelled on a road by any such vehicle does not exceed in the aggregate six miles in any one week.

4. A motor vehicle constructed or adapted primarily for the carriage of passengers and their effects, and any trailer drawn by it, while being so used.

[5. and 6. Deleted]

7. A vehicle which is being used for funerals.

8. A vehicle which is being used for police, fire brigade or ambulance purposes.

9. A vehicle which is being used for fire-fighting or rescue operations at mines.

10. A vehicle on which no permanent body has been constructed, which is being used only for carrying burden which either is carried solely for the purpose of test or trial, or consists of articles and equipment which will form part of the completed vehicle when the body is constructed.

11. A vehicle which is being used under a trade licence.

12. A vehicle in the service of a visiting force or of a headquarters.

13. A vehicle used by or under the control of Her Majesty's United Kingdom forces.

14. A trailer not constructed primarily for the carriage of goods but which is being used incidentally for that purpose in connection with the construction, maintenance or repair of roads.

15. A road roller and any trailer drawn by it.

16. A vehicle while being used under the direction of HM Coastguard or of the Royal National Lifeboat Institution for the carriage of life-boats, life-saving appliances or crew.

17. A vehicle fitted with a machine, appliance, apparatus or other contrivance which is a permanent fixture, provided that the only goods carried on the vehicle are:
    (a) required for use in the connection with the machine, appliance, apparatus or contrivance or the running of the vehicle,
    (aa) to be mixed by the machine, appliance, apparatus or contrivance with other goods not carried on the vehicle on a road in order to thresh, grade, clean or chemically treat grain,
    (b) to be mixed by the machine, appliance, apparatus or contrivance with other goods not carried on the vehicle in order to make fodder for animals, or
    (c) mud or other matter swept up from the surface of a road by the use of the machine, appliance, apparatus or other contrivance.

18. A vehicle while being used by a local authority:

    (a)   for road cleansing, road watering, snow-clearing or the collection or disposal of refuse, night-soil or the contents of cess-pools, septic tanks, or for the purposes of the enactments relating to weights and measures or the sale of food and drugs; or

    (b)   for the distribution of grit, salt or other materials on frosted, icebound or snow-covered roads or for going to or from the place where it is to be used for the said purposes or for any other purpose directly connected with those purposes.

19. A vehicle while being used by a local authority in the discharge of any function conferred on or exercisable by that authority under Regulations made under the Civil Defence Act 1948.

20. A steam-propelled vehicle.

21. A tower wagon or trailer drawn thereby, provided that the only goods carried on the trailer are goods required for use in connection with the work on which the tower wagon is ordinarily used as such.

22. A vehicle while being used for the carriage of goods within an aerodrome within the meaning of section 23(1) of the Airports Authority Act 1975.

23. An electrically propelled vehicle.

24. A showman's goods vehicle and any trailer drawn thereby.

25. A vehicle first used before 1 January 1977 which has an unladen weight not exceeding 1525 kilograms and for which the maximum gross weight, as shown on a plate affixed to the vehicle by virtue of Regulation 42 of the Motor Vehicles (Construction and Use) Regulations 1978 or any provision which that Regulation replaced, exceeds 3.5 tonnes but does not exceed 3½ tons.

26. A vehicle while being used by a highway authority for the purposes of section 160 or 200 of the Road Traffic Act 1972.

27. A vehicle being held ready for use in an emergency by an undertaking for the supply of water, electricity, gas or telephone services.

Qualifications Acceptable as Proof of Professional Competence

Taken from Appendix 7 to *A Guide to Goods Vehicle Operators Licensing (GV74)*. (Reproduced with the permission of the Controller of Her Majesty's Stationery Office.)

(a) For both a standard international and standard national licence:

(i) Fellow, or Member, of the Chartered Institute of Transport (in the road transport sector).

(ii) Fellow, Member, Associate Member, or Associate by examination, of the Institute of Transport Administration (in the road transport sector).

(iii) Member, or Associate Member, of the Institute of Road Transport Engineers.

(iv) Fellow, or Associate, of the Institute of the Furniture Warehousing and Removing Industry.

(b) For a standard national operator's licence only:

(i) Associate Member of the Chartered Institute of Transport (in the road transport sector).

(ii) Associates and Graduates of the Institution of Transport Administration, who are also at least 21 years of age, have at least 3 years' practical experience and hold the certificate of the National Examinations Board in Supervisory Studies (in the road haulage sector).

(iii) Associate of the Institute of Road Transport Engineers (by examination).

(iv) General or Ordinary Certificate in Removals Management issued by the Institute of the Furniture Warehousing and Removal Industry.

(v) Royal Society of Arts Certificate in Road Freight Transport granted on or after 1 May 1984 which specifically contains a footnote granting exemption.

Table of Appeal Cases

Table of Cases

Table of Statutes

Table of Statutory Instruments

Index